Spring
Δ

Montrose

SQUEHANNA
COUNTY

WAYNE
COUNTY

Δ Prompton

Honesdale ○

NEW YORK

Δ Lackawanna

Archbald
Pothole
Δ

LACKAWANNA
COUNTY

Scranton
○

Lake Wallenpaupack

Promised
Land
Δ

PIKE
COUNTY

Milford ○

Wilkes-Barre ○

eck

Δ   Δ Tobyhanna
Gouldsboro

MONROE
COUNTY

Δ
Big Pocono

Stroudsburg ○

Delaware River

Delaware Watergap
National Recreation Area

Δ Hickory Run

Δ
Lehigh Gorge

CARBON COUNTY

Jim Thorpe ○

Δ
Beltsville

NEW JERSEY

Lehigh River

PENNSYLVANIA'S NORTHEAST

POCONOS, ENDLESS MOUNTAINS, AND URBAN CENTERS

Pennsylvania's Northeast: Poconos, Endless Mountains, and Urban Centers
Text © 2000 by Ruth Hoover Seitz
Photography © 2000 by Blair Seitz
ISBN 1–879441–81–0
Library of Congress Control Number: 00–131371

Published by

RB
BOOKS

Seitz and Seitz, Inc.
1006 N. Second St.
Harrisburg, Pa 17102-3121
717-232-7944
FAX: 717-238-3280
www.celebratePA.com
Printed in Hong Kong

Graphic Design by
Klinginsmith & Company

PENNSYLVANIA'S NORTHEAST

POCONOS, ENDLESS MOUNTAINS, AND URBAN CENTERS

RB BOOKS

"...richly beautiful"

HARRISBURG, PA

RUTH HOOVER SEITZ

PHOTOGRAPHY BY BLAIR SEITZ

INTRODUCTION-SHAPED BY BLACK DIAMONDS

From our hilltop street in Palo Alto, a borough in Schuylkill County, I could count the piles of black slag beside a coal breaker dark and noisy on the far side of the Schuylkill River. Some time in the 1950s, steam shovels started scooping away the foliage behind our house and strip mining Sharp Mountain. The realm of coal framed the edges of my growing up world.

I learned early–and with fear and trembling–how to safely feed our basement furnace. After I put at least three shovels of hard, shiny anthracite on top of the bed of burning coals, I turned the shovel over and dug its edge into the heart of the mound of fuel. Flames would hiss and leap, licking the shovel. I knew that this safety measure would prevent gases from building into an explosive fire. I slammed the heavy iron furnace door shut and hung the shovel beside the coal bin, certain that no house fire caused by a faulty furnace would send the fire truck our way.

When I learned to "tend the furnace," American coal furnaces had been commonplace for more than a century. Much of the coal that was feeding them came from northeastern Pennsylvania where over 80 percent of the world's anthracite is found in three great coal fields. Heating homes with this "stone coal" emerged after Judge Jesse Fell of Wilkes-Barre modified a fireplace grate in 1808 to burn hard coal. The fuel's potential soared six years later when workers at a Philadelphia wire works discovered accidentally that a draft would keep the coal in an iron furnace burning with a sustained, smokeless flame. The risk-taking owners, Josiah White and Erskine Hazard, devised various methods of shipping coal down the Lehigh River to markets in the East.

One of their most ingenious operations was a gravity railroad on which cars of coal coasted nine miles from the mine at Summit Hill to the Lehigh at Mauch Chunk, now Jim Thorpe. Completed in 1827, it was the first railroad in Pennsylvania. In the century that followed, rail lines, coal mines, iron ore, and back-breaking immigrant labor combined to fuel the Industrial Revolution and to change the face of modern living.

Even our borough's grade school was blending ethnic differences among second-generation immigrants.

We still expressed our distinctiveness. Italian Catholics wore red for Saint Joseph and the Irish donned green for Saint Patrick. And we all shared some commonalities. Whether you were a Dobroshelsky, an O'Brien or a Genovese, you probably had a Nana from Europe living in your household. She spoke broken English but cooked pierogies, stromboli or chicken potpie–depending on her birthplace–that pleased any of your sledding or berry-picking pals. She was in charge until Mom returned from working in the textile factory. It was in this melting pot that I gained a fascination for the cultural baggage from which we humans construct our heritage. In Pennsylvania's northeast, people exercise a sense of belonging as well as pride in their ties to "the old country."

Hikes to pick huckleberries in the acidic tableland and blackberries at the edge of mine pits took me into a natural realm that hooked me on Pennsylvania's beauty. Early on, I distinguished mountain laurel from rhododendron and catbirds from mockingbirds. During my recent explorations, I have seen the results of enterprising commitment to ecological balance in reclaimed lands and preserved habitats. I shared the appreciation of

PAGE ONE: *Winter's snow and ice cover Bear Creek in Luzerne County.* PAGES TWO AND THREE: *On Pecks Pond in the Delaware State Forest, Pike County, a canoe rests on a dock.* ABOVE: *Mountain Laurel blossoms are the springtime attraction in Hickory Run State Park, Carbon County.*

local residents for restored city blocks and alive towns as well as thriving lakeside communities that treasure natural recreation areas.

The magnetism of the wild beauty in the northeast and the ethnic fervor of its natives combine to lure new residents and to spark creative ventures. It was local pride of so many people living and working in the northeast and the eagerness with which people shared their experiences that lit my own enthusiasm for the region's assets.

I thank the following for your helpfulness in the preparation of this book: Lori Miller of the Northeast Convention and Visitors Bureau, Scranton; Kelly Ruddick at the Pocono Mountains Vacation Bureau, Stroudsburg; Merle Mackin at Luzerne County Tourist Promotion Agency, Wilkes-Barre; Vivian McCarty and Shelly A. Stroud at Endless Mountains Visitors Bureau, Tunkhannock; and Sylvia Doyle, Carbon County Tourist Promotion Agency, Jim Thorpe. Invaluable for my exploration was the research of the staff at three of Pennsylvania's Heritage Regions–Delaware & Lehigh National Heritage Corridor, Bethlehem; Endless Mountains Heritage Region, Towanda; and Lackawanna Heritage Valley, Mayfield. I appreciated complimentary lodging at Days Inn Dunmore. I discovered much about the area from farm service agents, county planning commissioners, historical society directors and Pennsylvania state employees in respective bureaus in the following counties, all within the realm of this book–Bradford, Carbon, Lackawanna, Luzerne, Monroe, Pike, Schuylkill, Sullivan, Susquehanna, Wayne, and Wyoming.

What brought significance to my observations were people who personally shared information linked to their experiences and sent me off with a few more ideas. I thank you, Sister Adrian Barrett, Bob Baldassari, Peggy Bancroft, Sally Bohlin, Jim Boyle, Ken Brett, Sandra Chestnut, Jean Clocker, Owen Costello, Ralph J. Coury, Dan Cusick, Christopher L. DiMattio, Tom Fasshauer, Lynne Fay, Pam Fedak, Joe Fuller, Bob Gaetano, Christine Gray, Bill Halainen, Karen and Tom Hallowell, Kenneth Hawk, Florence Howanitz, Danadee Miller-Boyle, Bernie and Debbie Innela, Herb and Mort Kaplan, John Keeler, Mary Celeste Kosco, Nancy Kschinka, Jon Lindgren, Karen Loeschorn, Gregory Lull, Tom and Betty Lou McBride, Agnes T. McCartney, Drs. James and Nancy Merryman, Mary Ann Moran, Larry Newman, Louise Ogilvie, Kevin O'Hara, Dolly Petrilyak, Thomas Potter, Genevieve Logan Reese, Matthew L. Reiprich, Lindsay Robinson, Karen Rogowicz, Jim Rosselli, Jeff Rubel, Robert Sanchez, Ron Sheehan, Vaughn Shinkus, Kelly A. Stanton, Father Cassian Yuhaus, and Don and Ginger Zurflieh. Your generosity in sharing your time, knowledge, and resources enabled the text and photographs of this book to evolve.

–Ruth Hoover Seitz

CONTENTS

A Land of Surface Beauty and Underground Wealth

As a quadrant of the Keystone State, the northeast is a place of paradox. It offers easy access to big-city markets and comfortable hideaways within scenic wilds. Three interstates directly link this region to New England and the Midwest. I-80's Delaware River Bridge carries 43,000 vehicles each day. Some of those cars are on an escape route. In two-and one-half hours, inhabitants of the Great Megalopolis can flee the congestion of 30 million people and be hiking in a rhododendron thicket that also is home to black bear.

Here history repeats itself, but for different reasons. In the 19th century, the region's anthracite coal wooed thousands of immigrants to fuel America's Industrial Revolution. At the rise of the 21st century, the area's scenic beauty and low crime rates attract newcomers to what has become the fastest-growing area of the commonwealth. In the 1800s, before air travel took tourists to distant climes, summer vacationers fled eastern cities for a stay in these cool, refreshing mountains. By train and stagecoach they came to the Poconos, some drawn by Bushkill, the Watkins Glen of the Delaware, and others farther west to Jim Thorpe, America's Little Switzerland. Now families rent a resort condo for skiing and tubing in the winter and water sports and golf in the summer. But many are so drawn to the lifestyle of this scenic domain with its low price tag that they relocate.

There are wide variations within the 11 northeast counties. The downtowns of the region's two largest cities, Scranton and Wilkes-Barre, provide shopping, libraries, colleges, restaurants, and fun events, all within walking distance. Yet two counties, Bradford and Sullivan, have more cattle than people. Rural Pike County's population has increased by more than 50 percent each decade since the 1970s. Realtors in the Poconos claim they are "up to our ears with work" as people leave urban pressures in New York and New Jersey to adopt Pennsylvania's countryside. These new residents see deer in their backyards on weekends and board a Martz bus each workday to head to a Manhattan office or a New Jersey firm. Those living closest to the metropolitan areas of the northeast catch a train across the Delaware River in Port Jervis, New York, or drive a daily commute totaling five hours. They live in lakeside communities with names such as Pocono Mountain Lake Estates and Wild Acres, settlements that were carved out of forests.

While people develop new suburbs in the heart of the Poconos, they also safeguard the rich natural resources that first attracted vacationers to these mountains in the 1830s. At least half of Monroe County is fully- or partially-protected land. Throughout the area—from Wayne in the northernmost corner to Schuylkill, the southernmost part of the anthracite region, and north to Bradford along the New York border—conservancies and governments preserve and maintain scenic wonders and natural habitats.

Lehigh Gorge State Park protects park land for hiking and biking along a 30-mile abandoned railbed and water for rafting and canoeing, some in Class III whitewater. The river that was once an industrial resource moving coal to

ABOVE: *I-81 is a north-south interstate highway that traverses the northeastern quadrant of Pennsylvania, linking New York and Virginia and points beyond. These Schuylkill County mountains hold veins of anthracite with tilled fields in the valley stretching below the ridge.* **RIGHT:** *The lifestyle of early settlers in 1830 is depicted at Quiet Valley Living Historical farm, Stroudsburg.*

market, is now a state park set aside for topnotch recreational adventure.

The area's distinctive beauty and underground resources are a result of its geology. Eons ago, in fact, several hundred million years, the interaction of heat, moisture and pressure resulted in the formation of Pennsylvania's coal, limestone, shale, and other rocks. Other dramatic changes resulted in shifting, colliding, folding, and weathering so that now worn mountains and their intervening valleys lay in a northeast to southwest direction across this region. The lower boundaries of Monroe, Carbon and Schuylkill counties are marked by the Blue Mountain and Kittatinny Ridge, the path of the famed Maine-to-Georgia Appalachian Trail and the favored air route of migrating raptors.

North and west stretches an elevated plateau of hard sandstone, a tableland averaging 1,500 feet above sea level. It is known as the Poconos here; farther west, it is the Endless Mountains. Streams follow the downward slope of the earth, carving grooves in a surface that has flattened rock layers underneath.

Many surface features of the Pocono plateau are remnants of glaciation that began about 2 million years ago, when a mass of ice spread south from Canada. The last was the Wisconsin glacier, an ice sheet that covered the whole region, melting and retreating more than 12,000 years ago. The glacial lakes, swamps, falls, and peat bogs all result from melt and erosion across an expansive highland. Water scooped out the world's largest pothole, Archbald Pothole, north of Clarks Summit, and scoured out the smooth basins that have made a water playground of Seven Tubs Natural Area in Luzerne County. A sea of rocks known as Boulder Field in Hickory Run State Park in Carbon County is also a monument to the last glacier.

Water is abundant in Pennsylvania's northeast. Springs bubble into picturesque streams and tranquil lakes. Wayne, the northernmost county, features the most—more than a hundred natural and artificial lakes. The largest of the region, Lake Wallenpaupack, meanders with 52 miles of shoreline. In the town of Milford in Pike County, the town's water supply boasts a million surplus gallons each day.

Driving Interstates 80 or 84, east-west thruways, confirms the northeast's unspoiled wildness. Just off I-84 from Exit 7 spreads almost 3,000 acres of state forest called Bruce Lake Natural Area. Within this huge tract winds an extensive trail system that takes hikers and cross-country skiers through a

natural bog. Within the 14,400 Pocono acres that The Nature Conservancy (TNC) has protected is the state's largest concentration of globally rare species. In Long Pond, also the address of the Pocono Raceway, which lures more than 100,000 fans to NASCAR events, I saw rhodora (Rhododendron canadense), a magenta wild azalea, growing in a heath barren. This Pocono habitat is valued by TNC as one of the world's "Last Great Places."

This forested promised land was once the domain of 40,000 Lenape Indians. When governmental efforts such as Sullivan's March pressured the Lenapes to leave their settlements, some went west and others disappeared into rural communities, blending easily because the appearance of these Native Americans was not distinctive. Place names remind northeasterners today how closely these early residents related to the land. They themselves had not named places, but when European settlers asked for their names, the Lenapes offered descriptions in their language. For them "Poconos" is a "stream between mountains." Wyoming is the "great valley" stretching out from the Susquehanna, where an early settler found the soil "deep, strong, fat black, and fine, exceedingly kind and warm." Before the Pennsylvania Power & Light Co. dammed it to create a 15-mile-long lake, "Wallenpaupack" was a creek characterized as "deep, still water" by Native Americans. Along its shores is Lacawac Sanctuary, a preserve with the Indian name for "fork," and harboring one of the purest glacial lakes, Lake Lacawac.

Farther west, kayakers and canoeists go downriver on the North Branch of the Susquehanna, putting in at Sugar Run (Bradford Co.). Dave Buck of Endless Mountains Outfitters says paddling quietly downstream is a great chance to observe wildlife unobtrusively. Seeing eagles fly upriver or otters surface is a great display of wild beauty. In view of a boater, an osprey once swooped onto a fish dropped by an eagle.

In Sullivan County, nature reigns, with only one traffic light in the whole county, in Dushore. Driving east on Pa. Route 87 on a brilliant October day was like moving across an autumn palette. Each hilltop was a mixture of muted reds and yellows, the brightness of each crown varying with shade and sunlight. Woods along the roadside were carpeted by hay-scented ferns that had turned yellow true to their name. Each bend of the two-lane road led to a new scene of color, a diffusion of beauty unrivaled in forest culture. At times my car would swoop under a glowing yellow canopy. Then it would pass a cluster of hard-woods boasting of reds mixed with green conifers. Rising from a dip in the road, I glanced in the rear view mirror and caught an array of softer, blended hues in the receding Endless Mountains.

Some of the region's unique resources are the northern hardwood trees that create this dynamically

ABOVE: *Since the early part of the 20th century, the Poconos have extended the image of a place to relax. During a getaway, visitors cherish fine foods at resorts. This entree was served at the French Manor Inn.*
RIGHT: *Vacationers enjoy adventure sports such as kayaking or rafting in the white waters of the Lehigh River.*

brilliant foliage each fall. People come in droves to enjoy the autumn scenery. As the nights become cooler and shorter, it is the nature of deciduous trees growing in a temperate zone to lose the chlorophyl that makes their leaves green.

In their true colors, various species turn predictable hues. Early in the season the white ash becomes a deep purple and the American beech a rich yellow. Eventually the leaves of both become brown and drop. The winning combination, according to several foresters, is the sugar maple and red maple. Foliage of the first ranges from brilliant gold to deep red, sometimes in the same leaf. Red maples turn bright scarlet. The late-turners are the yellow-leafed aspens and the larch or tamarack, which is the only deciduous conifer.

In the broad valleys of Pennsylvania's Northeast–the Conyngham, the Wyoming, the Lackawanna, and the Delaware–agriculture thrives, but not without threat. Farmers in Luzerne County compete with developers for choice land in the scenic Conyngham so visible from Interstate 81 near Hazleton. Pittston, the "tomato capital," provides warm days and cool nights and a silt-loam soil that together produce a high-quality tomato. Harvested green from non-irrigated fields, the tomatoes go to a ripening room before being shipped throughout the East through October. Dairy farmers in the rich floodplain of the Delaware plant extra corn for the deer.

Agricultural extension officers in all 11 counties see farmers adding services to the usual farm products. Some feature entertainment such as haunted hayrides and corn maizes. Others offer "pick your own fruit" or produce Christmas trees.

Winter here characteristically offers 40-50 inches of snow each year. Pennsylvania's northeasterners expect it and enjoy the sports that thrive on it. Cross-country skiing, snowmobiling, and old-fashioned sledding excite visitors and residents. In Sullivan County there are 50-mile sled dog races near Forksville and a toboggan run at Eagles Mere, both dependent on nature's cooperation.

Here ice carving has developed into an outdoor entertainment. Kevin MacDonald, a native of Mountaintop, pioneered ice sculpture in this area in 1975. MacDonald's elaborate forts and castles, some requiring up to 9 tractor trailer loads of ice, draw at least 10,000 people. Competitive ice carving also attracts crowds at Honesdale's Winter Carnival each February; at night people take a tour to see the sculptures lit with colored lights.

The northeast of Pennsylvania displays its scenic beauty all four seasons. Even during March, known locally as "mud month," a hike to the bluffs overlooking the Delaware River is rewarding. Seeing eagles, hawks, or other raptors gliding northward is an uplifting sight worthy of braving the cold winds, notes naturalist John Serrao who guides aficionados of the outdoors in his native Poconos.

RIGHT: *Looking east, an aerial view of Mt. Tammany in New Jersey (left) and Pennsylvania's Mount Minsi (1,463 feet) accentuates the Delaware Water Gap, the result of millions of years of the earth's twisting and weathering.* **BELOW RIGHT:** *The trail along Fall Brook looks down on this waterfall and three others in 400-acre Salt Spring State Park, Susquehanna County.* **BELOW LEFT:** *In Ricketts Glen State Park, Luzerne County, hikers follow the course of Kitchen Creek as it drops almost 1,000 feet in a series of 22 waterfalls. At 94 feet, Ganoga is the highest.*

ABOVE: *A platform over Tannersville Cranberry Bog provides an autumn view of Cranberry Creek flowing through this 150-acre wetland, a National Natural Landmark in Monroe County.* **TOP RIGHT:** *The Bruce Lake Natural Area of Promised Land State Park is available only by foot to preserve the wildlife within the forest cover and swamp, valuable Pocono habitats.* **RIGHT:** *Early morning frost coats vegetation at Spruce Swamp in Lackawanna State Forest, of southern Lackawanna County.* **NEXT PAGES:** *Canyon Vista in Sullivan County's World's End State Park looks down from 1,750 feet onto Loyalsock Creek Gorge and the Endless Mountains.*

LEFT: *Men fly-fish on Tunkhannock Creek, also a resource for science students of Keystone College. Five trails with self-guides are open for creekside hiking.* **BELOW RIGHT:** *Farm fields stretch out on the floor of Schuylkill County with intervening forested ridges, all east of I-81.* **BELOW:** *Driving U.S. Route 6, a scenic 400-mile east-west road through Pennsylvania and beyond, affords stops at such natural beauty spots as Shohola Falls, Pike County. Warbler song filled this spring stop.* **NEXT PAGES:** *Snow-laden hemlocks and icy cascades such as Buttermilk Falls near Bear Creek in eastern Luzerne County create winter beauty in the water-rich region.*

LEFT: *For more than 20,000 years, rocks at Boulder Field in Hickory Run State Park have covered an area 400 feet by 1,800 feet without vegetation.*
BELOW: *Promised Land State Park represents the pristine scenery of Pike County. One-third of this county is government-protected land.*

BELOW: *Milk and veal production top the output of Bradford County farms. Maple products also come from the veins of the area's hardwoods.*
RIGHT: *Just 10 miles north of Scranton, Lackawanna State Park offers lake and stream fishing for both cold and warm water species.* **FAR RIGHT:** *U.S. Route 6 crosses the landscape of the Poconos, a plateau of forests, streams, and lakes. The cut in the forest is a trout stream widening into Shohola Falls, a dam, and Shohola Lake, Pike County.* **BOTTOM:** *High Knob Overlook in Wyoming State Forest, Sullivan County, offers this vista of the mountaintops of seven counties.*

REMNANTS OF INDUSTRIAL HISTORY

It was a find that took northeastern Pennsylvania to the forefront of America's Industrial Revolution–black rocks that burned long with a smokeless flame. This new fuel, anthracite coal, also burned hot. Underground deposits lay in distinct fields covering an area of 484 square miles in a northeast-southwest direction from Forest City in eastern Lackawanna County to Tower City in western Schuylkill County.

With the technology to mine it from steeply pitched veins that were often below the water table came new industries and a demand for workers. Coal fueled iron-making. And then it heated homes and spurred railroading. Getting it to where it could be used created new industries. Canals. Steam loco-motives and other railcars. Breakers for sorting coal and buildings for business offices. Mansions for the investors and patch towns for the miners. Educational institutions such as the Mining and Mechanical Institute in Freeland, the Johnson Technical Institute in Scranton, and the world's largest correspondence school (ICS), now Harcourt Learning Direct, in the same city were founded for miners during coal's heyday.

From the 1870s to the 1920s, anthracite was king. But early in the century, its use as an industri-al fuel dropped in favor of soft coal. After World War I, oil gradually replaced coal as a heating fuel, and, overall, national demand for coal slacked off. By 1950, less than half of the 175,000 miners who had been working in 1930 were still on the job. In 1959, the Knox Mine disaster resulted in wide-spread flooding of the mines in the Wyoming Valley. Another 7,500 men lost their jobs. The land above the deep mines was spoiled by acidic runoff, culm banks and strip mines. These environmental ail-ments cried for attention.

The region struggled for new income sources and communities cooperated to reclaim polluted coal lands. For example, adjacent to Luzerne County Community College in Nanticoke, Earth Conservancy removed black mounds of coal refuse and replanted grass to make the land useful again. In another area, artificial wetlands diluted the iron toxicity of mine drainage. In Schuylkill County, the Coal Lands Office is refilling "stripping holes" that scar the terrain and attempting to restore the land's original contours. Many of the structural remnants of mining, iron-making, and railroading are now attractions that educate the present generation.

The Lackawanna Coal Mine Tour in Scranton's MacDade Park is the real McCoy. A functioning mine between 1959 and 1966, No. 190 Slope took coal out of West Mountain. Since the mine reopened as a tourist attraction in 1985, more than three-quarters of a million visitors from all 50 states as well as 27 countries have discover-ed what miners in Pennsylvania's northeast experienced working in the bowels of the earth.

Daylight disappears as each tour group descends in a coal car to the bot-tom of the slope. The sur-prising depth–250 feet–is equivalent to the height of a 25-story building. At that depth, tourists spend an hour "walking in a miner's shoes," learning about the hazards of

ABOVE: *A miner had to bring in 2-3 carloads of hard coal a day. Each of the cars, as exhibited in the Anthracite Heritage Museum, Scranton, held about five tons of coal.* **RIGHT**: *As the Industrial Revolution boomed in America's northeast, railroads developed into the chief transportation system for hauling anthracite and other products.*

tunneling through rock to reach the seam of coal deep within the earth.

In this slope mine, dynamiting, picking, and loading coal carried life-threatening risks. To avoid flooding, there was the constant need to pump groundwater out of the mine. Pumping ceased when a mine closed down, and, unfortunately, its water poured into nearby mines.

For ventilation, miners needed fresh air circulating through all passageways. From the gangway or main route underground, miners dug perpendicular chambers, supported them with timber, and then blasted a crosscut every 60 feet to the right and left. The darkness and dampness added to the frustration of working for 8-10 hours in quarters that were often too shallow for standing. At the end of a working day a miner and his helper may have loaded a car with five tons of coal, but the air surrounding them was dust-choked, always carrying the threat of dangerous gases.

Schoolchildren on tour are shocked that kids worked in this unpleasant environment a century ago. Boys as young as eight opened the doors underground. At the age of 10, these nippers advanced to mule drivers, leading the animals pulling the coal cars. Above ground, six-to eight-year-old youngsters sorted coal, their hands cold and bleeding in their first mining job.

At the adjoining Pennsylvania Anthracite Heritage Museum are exhibits that explain the culture of the European immigrants who gravitated to the northeast's hard coal country to mine or to work in other industries that emerged. Looking at an exhibit on the textile companies that hired miners' wives, I overheard a woman point out to her children a lace machine "just like the one your grandmother worked on in the factory."

I also toured Ashland's Pioneer Tunnel Coal Mine, where a horizontal drift mine burrows 1,800 feet into the side of Mahanoy Mountain. Afterwards, I rode a steam "lokie" around the mountain to see a former strip mine with its gaping hole in the earth created when the surface coal was dug by a steam shovel.

Anthracite on the surface near the powerful Roaring Brook in Lackawanna County provided fuel and waterpower, two essentials to process iron ore. The company that launched this new venture in the mid-nineteenth century, the Lackawanna Iron Furnaces, attracted the labor and capital that founded Scranton.

Today, a stone's throw from the Lackawanna Station stand four stacks of the Scranton Iron Furnaces, America's only existing 19th century stone blast furnace stacks. They are silent remnants of the once hot, dusty, and noisy Lackawanna Iron & Coal Company. From 1847 to 1902, this enterprise produced pig iron that was made into T-rail and shipped throughout the northern hemisphere for rail track construction.

To learn about the initial challenges of producing and marketing pig iron, I dropped by the Visitors Center of the Scranton Iron Furnaces. The Lackawanna Iron and Coal Co. and its successor, Lackawanna Iron & Steel Co., were technological trailblazers, making steady improvements in smelting. Over the companies' 62 years of operation, the proprietors used the three primary fuels that were utilized over the ages to melt iron—charcoal, anthracite, and coke.

To get workers to isolated mines, companies built small settlements known as patch towns. Built in 1874 near a colliery, Eckley Miners' Village, as run today by the Pennsylvania Historical and Museum Commission, is a "patch" of 50 or so dwellings that shows the life of anthracite miners. Economic strati-

fication is obvious here with the mine owner's house the largest, with exterior decorations, and the small homes of second-class miners, the workers at the bottom of the pay scale, having no porch. A tour of a mining family's clapboard home reveals how new immigrants lived about 1890. During "Patch Town Days," an annual weekend celebration of ethnic traditions in anthracite country, I watched soapmaking and quilting and met Rich Pawling portraying miner Frank Kehoe looking coal-dirty at the end of a shift.

Scrubbing coal grime made washtub laundry a backbreaking chore. By 1924, men wanted the town electrified so that they could get washing machines for their wives. Such priorities accompanied improved miners' wages due to unionizing by the United Mineworkers (UMW). An exhibit in Eckley's Visitors Center illustrates how the UMW's John L. Mitchell organized mine workers into a powerful labor force. Beloved by miners for building solidarity and negotiating with management, Mitchell is commemorated in a monument in Courthouse Square in downtown Scranton.

Once a city with seven rail companies, Scranton is an apt location for Steamtown National Historic Site. Like thousands of other visitors, I came to this 40-acre attraction to experience a bit of railroad history. The site's two museums explain the history and technology of the steam locomotive with many intriguing mini-exhibits. Its roundhouse, turntable, repair shops, and tracks occupy a portion of the once-busy railyard of the Delaware, Lackawanna and Western Railroad (DL&W). This site was the hub for the famed

LEFT: *Between 1850 and 1920, the population of Pennsylvania's five top anthracite-producing counties rose from 156,000 to 1,080,000. As king, coal wooed even 12-year-olds to work 10 hours a day as breaker boys removing pieces of slate by hand.* **RIGHT:** *Bob Davis, tour guide at the Lackawanna Coal Mine in MacDade Park, Scranton, shows the room and pillar system of mining a vein of coal that formed underground 350 million years ago.*

"Phoebe Snow," which traveled between Hoboken, New Jersey, and Buffalo, New York. A remodeling of this line in the early 1900s resulted in the building of two landmark structures that are still often photographed today. One, the Tunkhannock Creek Viaduct at Nicholson (1912-1915) in Wyoming County, is an impressively arched rail bridge with ten visible spans of 180 feet and two more of 100 feet tucked into the approach hills.

The other is the six-story Lackawanna Station, whose six columns and central clock safeguard Scranton. It initially served 12 passenger trains, but a decline in rail travel closed its doors in 1970 until they reopened as a hotel in 1983. Lavish buffets rather than waiting room seats are below its restored barrel-vaulted leaded glass ceiling. Faience tile panels of scenes along the Hoboken-Buffalo route complement the marble walls. Even making a phone call in the DL&W's former vault is a reminder of the splendor that the Industrial Revolution endowed on Pennsylvania's northeast.

Communities in the region did benefit from donations by industrial owners and investors. The Scrantons remained committed to their namesake city. The Lackawanna Iron & Coal Co., of which they were principal owners, provided the land for Courthouse Square. Coal money from the Joseph Albright family endowed Scranton's public library. In Freeland, Eckley B. Cox and his philanthropist wife, Sophia, funded the Mining and Mechanical Institute (MMI) to educate miners' children. In Hazleton High Acres, the Markle mansion has been Penn State University's Hazleton campus administration building since 1948. (Inside is the table where the Markles gathered for Sunday dinners; the development office once served as Mrs. Markle's dressing room.) Years before, Penn State set up its first satellite center in the Markle Bank downtown. The family donated the current Hazleton Area Public Library on North Church Street and more recently, acreage and an endowment to Penn State Hazleton. The family forefather, George B. Markle, designed the modern coal breaker, besides forming a coal company and other businesses in the mid-1800s.

Gone are the years when King Coal reigned, pumping good living into cities such as Hazleton, Pottsville, Scranton and Wilkes-Barre, as well as plowing profits into New York and Philadelphia.

Today one of the state's nine heritage regions, the Lackawanna Heritage Valley Authority, educates residents and visitors about anthracite's role in the economic and social fabric of the region. Once a stone considered so worthless that it could not be given away in Philadelphia, anthracite coal became a valued resource. From the 1830s to the 1920s, coal dramatically fueled industries, spurred transportation systems, and attracted immigrants from diverse ethnic backgrounds. Today, with fewer than 100 deep mines, mining no longer dominates the economic picture. Even though it is only a history lesson for most residents, the legacy of the coal industry reverberates throughout the region.

RIGHT: *These arches of brick and stone are remnants of the Scranton Iron Furnaces built 1841-1857, near Roaring Brook in Scranton. A tour of the furnaces and a visitors center reveals how iron-making here rolled out the railroad rails of a nation.* **BELOW:** *A coal breaker rising above houses, this one at Ashley, was once common in the major anthracite-producing counties–Lackawanna, Luzerne and Schuylkill.*

ABOVE: *Lace and silk mills opened in the anthracite region to utilize the existing transport systems, coal as fuel, and an available female workforce. On display at Scranton's Anthracite Heritage Museum, this loom was set to weave Nottingham lace.* **FAR RIGHT:** *An engineer works at the restoration of a steam locomotive in the locomotive repair shop at Steamtown National Historic Site, Scranton.* **RIGHT:** *Children learn about coal mining from exhibits at any of the area's five anthracite museums and two mine tours in Scranton and Ashland. This photograph by George Harvan greets tourists at the Visitors Center at Eckley Miners' Village, Luzerne County.*

ABOVE: *A Catholic icon or image of a saint was usually on display in a coal mining family's home. This typical kitchen is one of the exhibits at the No. 9 Mine "Wash Shanty" Anthracite Coal Mining Museum, Dock Street, Lansford in Carbon County.* **RIGHT:** *Mining companies built "patch towns" such as Eckley, in the 1800s, so that miners could live close to their work.*

RIGHT: *The headquarters of coal-related companies reflected the power of these firms. Hudson Coal Company used this imposing structure on Wyoming Avenue for offices in Scranton. Now, as Finch Towers, the building is residential apartments. From the 1870s to the 1920s, the anthracite industry influenced the lives of most people in the region.* **BELOW RIGHT**: *The Delaware, Lackawanna and Western Railroad built this Tunkhannock Viaduct to span a valley more than half a mile wide and reduce a train's travel distance. Its arches tower 240 feet above the Tunkhannock Creek. It is in the borough of Nicholson, Wyoming County.* **BELOW**: *This monument in Scranton's Courthouse Square honors labor leader John L. Mitchell (1870-1919). As United Mine Workers president, he organized the miners into a unified force that altered the anthracite industry and solidified the labor movement.*

RIGHT: *Many churches in northeastern Pennsylvania grew out of ethnic communities. St. Patrick's Catholic Church in Wilkes-Barre's Rolling Mill Hill neighborhood was built in the 1930s by a largely Irish parish.* BELOW RIGHT: *The Hickory Street Presbyterian Church stands stalwartly in a south Scranton neighborhood.* BELOW: *Today the Wyoming Valley is a string of contiguous boroughs and cities along the Susquehanna River. U.S. Route 11 (bridge on left) spans the river at Pittston on the east shore and the borough of West Pittston.*

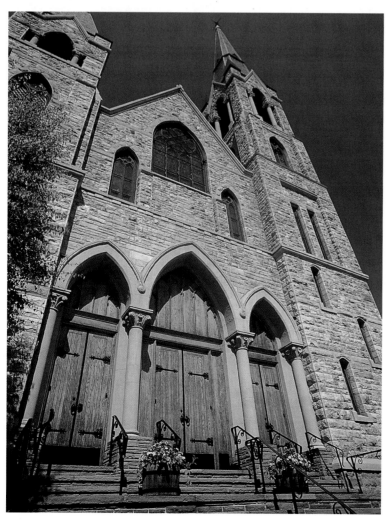

RIGHT: *The Holy Trinity Orthodox Church in McAdoo, Schuylkill County, features an icon screen, the Byzantine design.* **BELOW:** *St. Mary's Protection Byzantine Catholic Church on Chestnut Street in Kingston served Carpatho-Rusins as far back as 1887.*

THE POCONOS, A RECREATIONAL HAVEN

The Poconos became a recreational destination early, as soon as stagecoaches could bring travelers from eastern cities. By the mid-1800s large frame hotels accommodated guests who were panting for mountain coolness and relaxation. At first, Delaware Water Gap, a town that features trolley tours today, was the destination of vacationers, but railroads soon took travelers as far west as Mauch Chunk.

On a relief map on the ground floor of the library of Wilkes University, the Pocono Mountains are small, rounded knobs threaded by creeks all flowing southeast toward the Delaware River. The land's descent of 1,000 feet, sometimes gradual, sometimes steep, invites those streams to become cascades. Numerous falls, including Pennsylvania's highest, Raymondskill, draw visitors to the Delaware Water Gap National Recreation Area, which encompasses rivers, streams and mountains set aside for enjoyment. The heart of this park shared by New Jersey and Pennsylvania is the river running through it, the scenic Delaware, one of the last free-flowing rivers in the eastern United States.

The parameters of the Poconos are loosely defined, stretching from the Delaware west to the Lehigh River, then south to the Blue Mountain and north towards the New York border.

Fishing for carp, smallmouth bass, muskellunge, and walleye is great in the Delaware, also a source of water for 10% of the country's population. In May, shad swim upriver to spawn, a reality because dam-building plans were scrapped in the 1970s. Today, Delaware Water Gap National Recreation Area's 70,000 acres are visited by more than 5 million people annually.

Some visitors cross-country ski near old slate pits at Slateford Farmhouse, but most head to the park in summer. Swimming and barbecuing on the river's beaches are choice hot-day activities of city residents. Ardent hikers climb Pennsylvania's Mt. Minsi or New Jersey's Mt. Tammany, the highest points of the park,

to see the 400-foot-wide gap carved by nature between them. Rock climbers travel to Point of Gap Overlook on U.S. Route 611 to scale this breathtaking site at the river's tight "S" curve through Kittatinny Ridge.

A special place for learning about nature is the Pocono Environmental Education Center (PEEC) in Dingmans Ferry. People of all ages come to this former honeymoon haven to explore a rich diversity of natural habitats and species. For 24 hours, I experienced some of the fun offerings of this 38-acre campus within the National Recreation Area.

As soon as I checked in within view of bright nature posters and artwork, an intern invited me to hike one of PEEC's five self-guiding trails, this one through an upland deciduous forest and a hemlock grove. Along Scenic Gorge Trail I observed a tree with rectangular holes made by a pileated woodpecker. In the printed guide I learned many tree facts; for example, hemlocks can survive in as little as one or two inches of soil.

Under the guidance of a water instructor, several fifth graders and I took a canoeing lesson. Before we used our skills in a game of tag, we discovered a water snake near the pond's edge. After dinner we talked about bats, particularly the 11 species native to Pennsylvania and why six of them are endangered. Later the kids visited PEEC's bat boxes.

At breakfast, naturalist Steve Hawk had

ABOVE: *The clean and scenic Delaware River, the boundary between Pennsylvania and New Jersey, also marks the eastern border of the Pocono Plateau, here at Dingman's Ferry Bridge.* **RIGHT:** *Although seldom seen, black bears reside in all 11 of the counties of northeast Pennsylvania.*

already identified more than 30 bird species on his walk to the dining room. Yellow warblers nest in the dogwood shrubs.

PEEC's sensory trail offers a nature experience without sight. In the morning, blindfolded middle schoolers held onto a rope to guide their walk along the quarter-mile trail. Among other observations, they noticed changes in air temperature; their skin felt cooler in the shade and at the bottom of a small ravine.

An earlier walk was more exciting because a young black bear appeared on a trail that they had crossed a few minutes before. "Awesome!" the kids concluded.

Besides customized group events, PEEC offers family weekends and senior elderhostels. Science professionals also study at PEEC, which can accommodate 420 attendees. It's no small bonus for the learners and staff to have meals and lodging provided on-site.

The National Park Service also protects a designated 73 miles of the boundary between Pennsylvania and New York as the Upper Delaware Scenic and Recreational River. Just north of its southern terminus in the town of Deerpark, New York, is a great vista from Hawks Nest Scenic Overlook. This Wild and Scenic River offers boating, swimming, tubing, and fishing from Hancock, New York, south to Mill Rift, Pennsylvania, a river corridor between the Catskills and the Poconos. The Upper Delaware's open waters welcome the largest wintering bald eagle population in the northeast United States. People driving along Pa. Route 97 in February may see our national birds roosting and fishing.

The Poconos' natural scenery made the area a getaway from the start. For instance, artist John James Audubon explored the forests surrounding the Lehigh River in 1829. In more recent decades, newlyweds favored the Poconos as a destination. By the 1960s, heart-shaped tubs and champagne towers became an option for honeymoon couples. Ads began calling the area the "Honeymoon Capital of the World."

But families have had an even deeper recreational stake in the Poconos by developing summer places.

Courtesy of Pa. Game Commission

Many a retiree can recount childhood summers at family cottages.

Each development venture has its individual beginnings. For example, three generations ago several Swarthmore College alumni purchased nearly 2,000 acres around a natural "lake in the clouds," as described by the original settlers known as Lenape. After young families from Philadelphia built lakefront cottages, it was customary for mothers and children to stay all summer, with fathers joining them on weekends. Over the decades recreation centers such as tennis courts and a golf course have evolved as well as policies that conserve the natural habitats surrounding this stream-fed lake.

Descendants of the original purchasers also enjoy this private lake as a place to make friends with the wilds and with like-minded people. Cottagers enjoy traditions–trail-clearing weekends, sail races, and picnics with awards for the biggest fish caught. They also return to favorite spots–a falls with an 80' drop and a forest floor of high ferns. There are numerous other privately-developed vacation or year-round communities, each thriving on the natural beauty of the Poconos and organized according to its own management structure.

Visitors who prefer to relax without any ownership commitment choose to stay at a resort. Golf is challenging at Woodloch Springs in Hawley and at Great Bear near Shawnee. At Fernwood Resort and Country Club and Buck Hill Falls Golf Club, the course architects devised intricate spots with natural features. Deer commonly appear on greens in the Poconos.

At Skytop Lodge, golf was also a priority when Robert White designed its championship course in 1925. Now guests enjoy a wide range of recreational activities at this elegant resort set among 5,500 wilderness acres. A children's day camp, a fly fishing school, a shooting range, and 30 miles of hiking trails provide outdoor experiences. Some guests prefer a foray into an undisturbed area with Skytop's naturalist, John Serrao. The bonus may be seeing some of the 300 species of wildflowers identified here or a striking view atop West Mountain.

In early spring, up to 10 different species of waterfowl paddle on Skytop Lake. This wildlife paradise is a favorite of beavers. Brook and brown trout, wily trophy species, are abundant in the fast-moving waters of Leavitt Branch, known by guests as the "Trout Stream." Room amenities include walking sticks and outlets at the desk lamp for computer hookup. At various levels of grandeur, facilities here and at other Pocono resorts serve family reunions as well as corporate meetings.

Dining merits a lot of attention at area resorts. Excellent French cuisine prevails at The French Manor, a stone chateau near South Sterling. The Manor, The Settlers Inn in Hawley and Cliff Park Inn in Milford are three Pennsylvania accommodations cited by Johansens Recommended Hotels and Inns in North America, Bermuda, and the Caribbean for luxurious ambience and traditional hospitality. Fireside dining on a winter night is pleasant at the Manor, which is nearly 2,100 feet above sea level. At The Chateau at Camelback, a cascading waterfall is a pleasant-sounding backdrop to a splendid view during mealtime.

On rainy days vacationers can shop at the Crossings, outlet stores, or one-of-a-kind places such as Marshall Creek's Huffman's, a general store open since the 1820s. The Poconos is known for candle shops, several making their own products. In fact, candle making is observable at American Candle in Bartonsville. This company, as well as Mountainhome Candle & Wicker have been manufacturing for more than 20 years. Country Candle Shoppe in Kresgeville is another stop for scented candles.

Product-packed environments are readily accessible, but any stay in the Poconos should include a walk through a bog, one of the region's unique habitats. At the trailhead of Tannersville Cranberry Bog in Monroe County, naturalist Karen N. Boyle defined the setting we would visit. "A bog has both herbaceous and woody plants, and this one is the southernmost bog in the country."

As we entered this National Natural Landmark via a boardwalk, we realized its age and sacredness. It has been evolving for hundreds of years from a lake of glacier melt. Plants grow on spongy sphagnum moss with peat moss underneath. Large clumps of sphagnum called hummocks float in this watery depth and become a mat that supports the growth of such flowers as swamp orchids, goldthread, and insect-eating pitcher plants.

Large shrubs such as highbush blueberry, swamp honeysuckle, and leatherleaf flourish in this acidic environment. Saffron-colored threads of daughter climb haphazardly over a thicket of swamp loosestrife. In the summer, bladderwort bloom yellow, and pickerel weed has rose flowers.

Larch or tamarack trees lift arms with soft needles that turn yellow in the fall. Since a bog is colder and wetter than its surroundings, life here is slow-growing. The trunk of a larch tree seven inches in diameter may be 100 years old.

Despite a prevailing eeriness in this liquid realm dense with plants, animals enjoy the environment. Bears, gray foxes, bobcats, and owls thrive here. For us humans, a permit or tour guide is needed to enter Tannersville Cranberry Bog. That fact and the setting itself convey a feeling of magic. A bog walk is a Pocono adventure worth booking.

Contrasts within the Poconos *au natural* are striking. In the Pohopoco State Forest very near

ABOVE: *Viewed from its mountain top restaurant, Camelback is a four-season resort just off I-80 in the heart of the Poconos.* **RIGHT**: *In the 1840s, John Roebling of Brooklyn Bridge fame designed the Delaware Aqueduct, "a canal above the water," to steer goods across the Delaware River safe from timber rafts and ice jams. Today, the aqueduct is a bridge between Lackawaxen in Pike County and New York.*

Long Pond, a trail for recreational ATVs heads across heavily forested ridges and then dips down to a treeless basin so cold that below-freezing temperatures have been recorded every month of the year. Is this a glacial flashback?

Seeing a bear in the wild is not unrealistic in the Keystone State's northeast. Bears have been sighted in all of the 11 counties between Schuylkill and Wayne, even in backyards. In Bear Creek, one has swiped ripe apples that dropped from a tree. Bears have been spotted on the golf course at Water Gap Country Club in Monroe County. Golf carts do not alarm bears because they have become used to them in the Poconos.

In Pennsylvania more than 10,000 black bears coexist with 12 million people. The state's nationally renowned bear expert, Gary Alt, finds it amazing that animals weighing up to 800 pounds can live in our forests and not be seen any more than they are. Bears hide out in swampy thickets of rhododendron, blueberry, and spruce. They also inhabit the thick underbrush of mixed hardwood forests, scarfing up acorns and berries before settling into dormancy in a den for several winter months.

Alt's efforts to tag and collar black bears have yielded invaluable information on their habits and habitat. In his 8,000 encounters with the bruins since 1974, this biologist has learned that they are non-aggressive, almost shy.

Their hibernation is far from dead-to-the-world sleep. In hibernation a bear's body temperature drops only seven or eight degrees. During their three-to-four months of winter rest, bears are aware but lackadaisical. They don't eat, drink, or eliminate wastes; preparing for mothering is top priority for the females.

The species' winter home is each animal's birthing place. Alt discovered that all cubs are born in January. His research also uncovered a biological phenomenon. Although bears mate with multiple partners from May through September, the fertilized eggs are not implanted into the uterus until late November or early December. A bear develops over a mere six weeks and is born in January weighing about 12 ounces curled up in a shape similar to a can of soda.

In Pennsylvania when food is abundant, litters most commonly have three cubs, but may have one or five. The little blue-eyed cubs stay with their mother for 1 1/2 years until they set off to raise their own families.

Harvesting black bears reduces their destruction of crops, livestock, and beehives. Since 1997, licenses to hunt bears have been sold at more than 1,000 sites throughout the state. Approximately a fifth of the state's bear harvest is taken in the counties of the northeast. Pennsylvania hunters target this mammal a few days in late November.

The northeast has wooed creative souls who have sparked beneficial endeavors with wide ripples.

From Honesdale since 1946 has come the successful magazine, *Highlights for Children.* Its editorial staff still answers the thousands of letters that children write each month, a practice that began three generations ago when Garry C. Ph.D and his wife Caroline Myers began publication.

The famed choral leader Fred Waring (1900-1984) broadcast his Pennsylvanians from Worthington Hall, now the Shawnee Playhouse in the charming community of Shawnee-on-Delaware. Writers, musicians, and other artists have cherished the secluded beauty of nature for both its inspiration and its privacy. Dick Smith, a resident of Honesdale, was inspired by Pocono winters to write "Winter Wonderland," a holiday music favorite enjoyed by people far away from the fireside coziness of a hideaway in the woods. Those forests, so inviting in any season, make a holiday rewarding.

Whether people come to the Poconos to vacation or to settle, they luxuriate in the sparkling streams between steadying mountains-always conscious of the proximity of city skyscrapers on the other side of the I-80 bridge.

LEFT: *Camelback Ski Area operates both day and night with a variety of slope challenges.* **BOTTOM LEFT:** *Skiers perfect their style at Big Boulder Ski Area in Blakeslee. In the 1950s, snowmaking was first introduced at this resort.* **BELOW LEFT:** *Geared to freedom of movement and style, snowboarders love terrain with bumps and jumps here at Big Boulder.* **BELOW:** *Snow tubing, an activity rather than a sport, is now popular at many Pocono resorts, but it was first introduced here at Jack Frost Mountain, Blakeslee, in Monroe County.* **NEXT PAGE:** *Snow coats hemlock boughs and rhododendron leaves along Pinchot Trail, a 23-mile loop in Lackawanna State Forest.*

TOP RIGHT: *The Settlers Inn at Bingham near Hawley is situated at the juncture of U.S. Route 6 and PA Route 590.* **BOTTOM RIGHT:** *Pocono accommodations range from the rustic to the elegant. The rooms at The Settlers Inn north of Lake Wallenpaupack Park hold "quiet comforts" for guests.* **BELOW:** *Resorts of the Poconos are nestled in the forests.*

ABOVE: *Dinner at the French Manor Inn on Huckleberry Mountain in South Sterling is bound to include one of the chef's special sauces.* **TOP RIGHT**: *New luxurious homes are going up in Pennsylvania's northeast, the fastest growing region of the Keystone State.* **BOTTOM RIGHT**: *Reading in the library is one of many guest amenities at Skytop Lodge, a luxury resort offering a wide range of entertainment activities with access to untouched wilderness.*

LEFT: *Couples enjoy romantic dining at any of numerous Pocono inns, lodges, and restaurants from Matamoras in Pike County to White Haven in Luzerne County.* **BELOW:** *In the western Poconos, a bed and breakfast such as "the Victoriann" on Broadway, Jim Thorpe's main street, gives tourists a Victorian atmosphere within walking distance of the borough's attractions.* **BELOW LEFT:** *Caesars Pocono resorts popularized honeymoon suites with 7 1/2 foot-tall champagne glass-shaped whirlpools.*

LEFT: *Fall brilliance in the Poconos stems from the abundance of sugar and red maples, Pike County.* ABOVE: *The stunning pinkish purple rhodora grows in a scrub barren near Long Pond, Monroe County.* RIGHT: *This wild azalea and close relative of the mountain laurel, the pinkster, is common in the Poconos' acidic habitat.*

BELOW: *Mountain laurel, the state flower, is prolific in the Poconos. The June blooms are abundant in areas of Hickory Run State Park, Carbon County.*
RIGHT: *Mountain laurel, an evergreen shrub, and hay-scented ferns thrive in the rocky, well-drained woodlands of the Poconos.* **BOTTOM**: *Blooming in July, after its relative, the mountain laurel, the rhododendron is an exquisite blossom.*

BELOW: *Dorflinger-Suydam Wildlife Sanctuary, in White Mills, Wayne County, welcomes nature lovers to its trails filled with birdsong in the spring.* **RIGHT:** *Shrubs of mountain laurel, abundant in many of the state parks of northeastern Pennsylvania, burst into bloom in early summer.* **BOTTOM:** *A series of waterfalls in Dingmans Creek are accessible from George W. Childs Recreation Site near Dingmans Ferry in the Delaware Water Gap National Recreation Area.*

PAGES 60-61: *Cascading 130 feet, Dingmans Falls is Pennsylvania's second highest falls, located down a short trail off U.S. Route 209 in the Delaware Water Gap National Recreation Area.* **LEFT:** *A bicyclist rests beside a falls in Bear Creek, a designated wild stream in Luzerne County.* **BELOW RIGHT:** *Canoeists paddle the Delaware River, one of the last undammed rivers in the East.* **BOTTOM LEFT:** *During water release weekends, rafters and kayakers take to the Lehigh River Gorge State Park class III whitewater in Carbon and Luzerne Counties.*

LEFT: *Boating is a prime recreation on 13 mile-long Lake Wallenpaupack in both Wayne and Pike Counties.* **BELOW:** *When the autumn leaves peak, such as here in Pike County, people take drives to enjoy the deep hues of the fall foliage.* **BELOW RIGHT:** *A man fishes on 250-acre Gouldsboro Lake in Gouldsboro State Park, Monroe and Wayne Counties.* **BELOW LEFT:** *Canada geese pass by rowboats pulled ashore until warm weather returns to Promised Land State Park, Pike County.*

SCRANTON

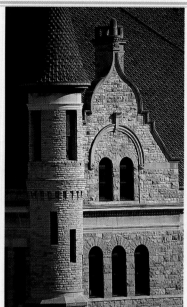

Even though a cold wind cuts across the path of pedestrians heading for the St. Patrick's Day parade, an expectant mood precedes Scranton's biggest downtown event. It is a homecoming of sorts. Locals who grew up going to this festive parade return to celebrate their heritage-and to relive their youth. Dressed in layers and mostly green, people stride purposefully to a prime viewing spot.

Once situated, some huddle in quilts. Others buy green balloons. By the time the band strikes up the national anthem, tens of thousands line the parade route that starts on Wyoming Avenue and ends at Washington Avenue. Outside of Farley's Pub, university students cluster five-deep for the day's special, kegs and eggs–green, of course.

But some come to be seen. Close to 6,000 people march in the parade, some as individuals. They sport an odd hat or carry a sign or flag. "It means so much to them!" explains John Keeler, one of the organizers whose own ties to the St Patrick's Day parade go back to a 1930 photo of his great-grandfather riding in an old car in the parade. "Being part of the parade fosters a feeling of belonging to something that's important."

The sun works as hard as the wind, but it never warms the aluminum bleachers on Linden Street. Marching bands and company floats entertain the crowd. Dancers from the Irish Cultural Society step high, and friends on the sidelines wave to the Lions from Minooka, an Irish section of Scranton. The crowd enthusiastically cheers pipe bands such as the Penn-York Highlanders and Sword of Light. Clowns and motorized units from Irem Temple are a favorite. Some marchers carry Ireland's flag.

In this parade, Scrantonians can flaunt their own interests and style. Clearly this parade is for "them that are Irish and them that wish they were Irish." Several dozen faces of varying tones wear "Friends of the Poor" sweatshirts and follow a short Catholic nun walking in green socks and carrying a shillelagh decorated with ribbons. Sister Adrian Barrett has been

"enhancing the quality of life in low-income neighborhoods" since 1971.

This spunky woman in her seventies calls being in the parade "a civic response or building a sense of belonging." Acknowledging that the parade includes a diverse group, Keeler insists that it celebrates the heritage of all of the area's ethnic groups as well as the Irish. Morning dissolves into afternoon and more waving red-cheeked marchers go by to the wail of bagpipes. Lynne Fay of Duryea keeps me supplied with her homemade shamrock cookies.

Afterwards, part of the crowd gravitates to the Scranton Cultural Center for more entertainment–in the warm. Friends greet each other like family as they buy scones. Some hold their plates for the potato stew; the sharp scent of boiled cabbage drifts over the crowd. Soon the velvet skirts of the Emerald Isle Step Dancers swirl across the wooden floor to the rhythmic tap of their black-strapped shoes. On their bodices are stitched the colors of both American and Irish flags–a true Scranton spirit.

Scrantonians have brandished their loyalty, their sense of belonging in fruitful ways. At the beginning of the 20th century, when the city was the industrial transportation hub of the East, the Delaware, Lackawanna & Western (DL&W) Railroad built a flagship train station. Through a concerted effort, this French Renaissance-style structure was restored in 1984 and is now the Radisson Lackawanna Station Hotel. It majestically greets all the cars that swoop into the downtown via the Central Scranton Expressway.

To the east, the University of Scranton's

ABOVE: *For the Lackawanna County Courthouse, West Mountain stone was turned into this Victorian chateau-style edifice.* **RIGHT:** *Horns of the Scranton High School Band perform at the St. Patrick's Day parade.*

hillside campus is a prominent feature of the city skyline. While "preparing men and women for others" in the Jesuit tradition, the university ranks consistently among America's Best Colleges, according to U.S. News & World Report. A family gift prompted the University of Scranton to relocate to its present site in 1942 when the scholarly Jesuits assumed leadership. The university, founded in 1888, moved to its present site in 1942 when the Society of Jesus (Jesuits) assumed leadership. The family of former Pennsylvania governor and U.S. congressman William W. Scranton donated their home, now a key administration building known as the Estate, to the school.

The Scrantons in America have engaged in entrepreneurship and public service for 10 generations. With roots in Connecticut, brothers George W. (1811-1861) and Selden T. Scranton (1814-1891) founded an iron-smelting company and the city that bears the family name. Other relatives added their expertise and financing to various industries including steel-making. Scrantonians do not overlook these contributions, even remembering that Governor William W. Scranton wasn't above picking up litter while walking downtown.

In 1857, a Scottish engineer named James Archbald arrived to plan the Delaware & Husdon Gravity Railroad for the Scrantons. His son-in-law, George H. Catlin, built a home across from the Scranton estate. Now known as the Catlin House and home of the Lackawanna Historical Society, this spacious dwelling of Tudor Revival style was considered "a show place" when it was built in 1912. A tour reveals flooring of inlaid oak parquet, fireplaces of Italian marble, and solid black walnut woodwork. In the early 1900s, the architectural stature of many Scranton structures rose with the city's industrial success. Besides splendid mansions and townhouses going up along such streets as Washington Avenue, public buildings brought people of various ethnic groups together. Today, many of those edifices are restored for new purposes and serve Scrantonians well.

For instance, Lackawanna Junior College, a state-of-the-art campus at 501 Vine Street training 1,000 students downtown, represents a $15 million rehab of the city's 1896 landmark Central High School. The first of the building's four stories was built of Indiana limestone, with the other floors of native yellow-bluff sandstone. An important aspect of the project in the late '90s was the restoration and upgrading of Central's ornate auditorium. In the 1920s, music lovers acclaimed its acoustics and roomy stage. Among the world-famous performers who played here were John Philip Sousa and his band and the Russian composer Sergei Rachmaninoff. Called the Mellow Theater since its completion in 1999, the 1,000-seat auditorium again hosts top performances.

Across the street and active day and evening is the Albright Memorial Library, a French Gothic building on grounds designed by the famed urban landscape architect Frederick Law Olmstead. Inside, stained glass windows with bookmark designs reflect soft hues on researchers at work under a barrel-vaulted ceiling in the second floor reference area. In 1889 the library initially bought 17,000 volumes by citizens' subscriptions. The grounds and the structure were donated by the family of Joseph Albright, a former Scrantonian.

Even people who have outgrown childhood like to slip into the adjacent children's library. The building's first life was as a Christian Science church. The present interior design makes it easy for youngsters to worship the learning that books and videos inspire. Cloud mobiles float in the high ceiling. Young audiences sit on carpeted stairs to enjoy a puppet show performed behind a facade of recognizable Scranton buildings.

The city's central architectural jewel is the Lackawanna County Courthouse in Courthouse Square. Standing like a chateau with striking towers, it is the dominant edifice in Scranton's downtown Gothic District.

Immigrants who built the Lackawanna Valley championed originality that still boosts the economy. In 1890, Thomas J. Foster responded to miners in need of a technical education by establishing study-by-mail courses. By the 1950s, International Correspondence Schools (ICS) was regarded as "the Harvard of home-study institutions." Today locals still refer to the world's oldest and largest correspondence school as ICS, even though this employer of 700 workers is now an international corporation called Harcourt Learning Direct. The school began in Finch Towers, now residential apartments at 424 Wyoming Avenue. In 1906, the Haddon Craftsmen Building on the same street rose to handle printing and other ICS needs. In 1921, ICS expanded to include a women's institute, which now houses Scranton Preparatory School. ICS alumni helped to design the current ICS facilities at 925 Oak Street in north Scranton. Over the decades the local economy has reaped multiple benefits from this endeavor.

Building use may change, but some cultural preferences hold firm. For dependable kosher fare hit Abe's Deli on Wyoming Avenue. Go to Cooper's for seafood and international beers served in a realm of historic memorabilia. There is only one worthy Texas-style weiner in Scranton; it's a chili hot dog from Coney Island Lunch, started by Steve Karampilos in the first quarter of the 20th century. One of the long-time favorite dance bands is "The Poets." If you thought the Welsh could live without music, you haven't been to one of their songfests in west Scranton.

Going for Old Forge pizza is a tradition in northeastern Pennsylvania. Following the lead of the prior generation, each family stays loyal to its favorite among the half a dozen Main Street pizzerias in Old Forge on the western side of Scranton. Don't expect a trace of Martha Stewart in the setting. The bars are dark with beer brands and a statue of the Virgin Mary in neon glow. Service is direct,

ABOVE: *Landscaped with benches and monuments, Courthouse Square in the heart of Scranton sets off the Lackawanna County Courthouse.* **RIGHT:** *University of Scranton students enjoy warm weather on the University Commons near the Student Center of this city campus.*

almost abrupt. "Okay, honey," shouts a pencil-thin waitress, serving patrons beer with a small turned-over glass wobbling on the top of each open bottle. After sampling several pizzas, I give high marks to Revello's double crust with a half-inch of oozing cheeses in the middle. Don't overlook Arcaro & Genell's red and white pizza, which made *U.S.A. Today's* Top 10.

This Italian neighborhood is near a world-renowned Roman Catholic shrine, St Ann's Basilica. It embodies just as much ceremony as the pizzerias do informality. Each year from July 17-26, thousands of devotees go up St. Ann's Street, a long grade, to gather for a "solemn novena" several times each day. These pilgrims petition St. Ann, the grandmother of Christ, for healing and favors. For this tradition, they light candles in a grotto and attend mass in the basilica, which seats 1,500 worshippers. Many more listen outside during the telecast services held each day up through the 26th, St Ann's feast day. Since 1925, the event has attracted people from around the country and world.

Parish members put just as much energy into church festivals that take place in their own churches once a year. For instance, each July at St. Rocco's in Dunmore, sandwiches of sausage and peppers are a big seller. This weekend event is only one of about 30 church festivals.

Despite strong traditions, this city of 75,000 is striving to develop into a vibrant city undergoing an urban renaissance. Scranton Tomorrow is an organization of local leaders actively upgrading the city's quality of life through a visionary plan of action. There is support for regional recreational trails, an inter-modal transportation system, and more "hang places" for youth. First Night™ Scranton, a family-focused cultural festivity, brings in the new year. Musicians, dancers, and other performers entertain at 15 downtown venues that are usually dark in the evening. The courthouses, both federal and county, are churches, and unoccupied buildings filled with action, light, sound, and an itinerant audience. Near

midnight, the crowd clusters downtown in front of the bridge spanning Lackawanna Avenue to watch fireworks set to music with a climactic countdown.

All year long, downtown shoppers head for the Mall at Steamtown, an indoor facility of retail stores, a food court, and an open walkway to America's only national historic site on steam railroading. It is understandable that one of the favorite stores here is devoted to toy trains.

An eight-block cultural district facilitates an easy walk to performances. A pivotal arts building, Scranton Cultural Center is the city's home for the Northeastern Pennsylvania Philharmonic, the area's symphony orchestra; for TNT, a professional group that performs original plays and seldom-acted classics; for the Ballet Theatre of Scranton and the Scranton Civic Ballet; for Scranton Community Concerts as well as for pottery, dance, and music studios. Arts groups benefit from the care that the Masons put into the acoustics and layout of their temple when they contracted Raymond M. Hood, architect of Rockefeller Center, to design the building in the 1920s.

Over several visits I gained warm appreciation for its details, including such art motifs as hearts, snowflakes, lilies, and oak leaves presented as decorative painting. After I opened the mirrored double doors to enter the ballroom, I was beneath a coffered ceiling rich in painted symmetry with nature tones. The center's theatres and lounge areas invite public and private events as Scranton's Masonic Temple regains its stance in the 21st century as an "active regional center for the arts."

This university city boasts many fine structures, including a downtown nucleus of Gothic architecture. Never ravaged by flood or deserted by residents, Scranton has buildings with a strong industrial history on which to build a new economic focus. The spirit with which its people march on St. Patrick's Day and feast at the Italian festival on Labor Day serves their efforts tremendously.

BELOW: *People line the route of Scranton's St. Patrick's Day parade to cheer the dozens of groups marching. This March event draws thousands, including former residents.* **RIGHT:** *The Classy Cruisers of Scranton entertain St. Patrick's Day crowds.* **BELOW RIGHT:** *At La Festa Italiana, feet dance enthusiastically to live music from the North Washington Avenue stage. Scranton's Courthouse Square welcomes the city's largest ethnic festival each Labor Day weekend.* **NEXT PAGES:** *Scranton High School Band marches in their hometown's St. Patrick's Day parade.*

TOP RIGHT: *The Beaux Arts style of the 1896 Scranton Electric Building holds distinction in "The Electric City" where the first electrically-powered trolley ran.* FAR RIGHT: *The Steamtown Mall is a downtown shopping complex with a walkway to Steamtown National Historic Site.* BELOW RIGHT: *City Hall's ornamental towers rise in the Gothic district.* BELOW: *Temple Israel, Gibson Street and Monroe Avenue, is one of five Scranton synagogues serving the six percent of the city's population that is Jewish.*

ABOVE: *Receptions are held in the eloquent Catlin House (1912), headquarters of the Lackawanna Historical Society. In the stairwell hangs a portrait of Governor William W. Scranton (b. 1917) by Jay Wesley Jacobs, on loan from the Scranton family.* **TOP RIGHT:** *Built in the 1770s by a settler from Connecticut named Isaac Tripp II, the Tripp House is Scranton's oldest house.* **BELOW RIGHT:** *The former home of engineer George H. and Mary Walsh Catlin, the Catlin House features black walnut woodwork, an onyx mantle clock, and a portrait of Sarah Augusta Templeton Frothingham Archbald (1805-1874), Mary Catlin's mother.*

TOP LEFT: *Females perform "The Complete Works of William Shakespeare (Abridged)," a production of TNT, Scranton Cultural Center's theater in residence committed to giving northeastern Pennsylvania audiences plays they don't get elsewhere.*
ABOVE: *Ornate details decorate the ceiling of the main auditorium of the Masonic Temple (1930) now the Scranton Cultural Center, a downtown venue for regional art performances.* **LEFT**: *Emerald Isle Step Dancers entertain in the ballroom of the Scranton Cultural Center after the city's famed St. Patrick's Day parade.*

ABOVE: *This Everhart Museum exhibit features Dunmore artist John Willard Raught (1857-1931) and sculpture "Sunrise-Sunset" (right) by local artist William Tersteeg.* **TOP RIGHT:** *The Everhart Museum in Nay Aug Park holds collections of fine art and natural history. In addition to Raught's art, the permanent collection includes Pennsylvania artist Violet Oakley (1874-1961) as well as Thomas Cole, Robert Henri and Andy Warhol.* **BOTTOM RIGHT:** *Art classes in the Junior Gallery at the Everhart fulfill the aim of the museum's founder, Dr. Isaiah Fawkes Everhart (1840-1911) to give "the young... pleasure and education."*

LEFT: *Courthouse Square is a downtown magnet for Scrantonians with the imposing Victorian-style Lackawanna County Courthouse (1884) as the focal point.* **TOP ABOVE:** *The grand lobby of the Radisson Lackawanna Station Hotel, formerly the main waiting room of the Delaware, Lackawanna and Western Railroad (1908), includes Carmen's, a four-star restaurant.* **ABOVE:** *The University of Scranton is one of 28 Jesuit colleges in the United States. On the University Commons, the sculpture "Metamoia," by Gerhard F. Bhut, depicts the spiritual transformation of Ignatius Loyola, founder of the Society of Jesus.*

WILKES-BARRE

Wilkes-Barre played a pivotal role in determining the size of the Keystone State. Would the cloud-topped mountains and dazzling rivers west of the Delaware Water Gap be part of Pennsylvania or Connecticut? Both were states for a quarter of a century before their disputed claims were settled in 1807. The boundary strife started in the Wyoming Valley, a three- to six-mile-wide "great plain" on both sides of the Susquehanna River, a rich flat-land that cradled Wilkes-Barre and adjoining small towns.

That was the destination of a group of Connecticut Yankees who wound their way westward through thick forests on Native American trails to take advantage of a land package offered in1755 by the Susquehanna Company. This private corporation offered five miles square along the river to groups of 40 settlers. But the land deal soured by 1774 because the new settlers provoked a conflict with the Pennamites, residents who claimed to be part of the colony of Pennsylvania. The Yankees won the first war. To strengthen their position, they laid out the town of Wilkes-Barre, naming it for John Wilkes and Isaac Barre, two of the most outspoken censors of the king's policies in Parliament. Fighting about overlapping land grants suspended when the Revolutionary War hit the valley in 1778.

On July 3, in the brutal Battle of Wyoming, Major John Butler and his Tory Rangers and Native American allies crushed the local militia and Continental soldiers. Remnants retreated to Forty Fort, the garrison that they had built.

In 1779, after this battle and and a subsequent massacre, President George Washington authorized a military expedition that became known as Sullivan's March. Their route began in Easton, continued west through the Poconos, eventually swooping down from Wyoming Mountain on a trail called Laurel Run, now a steep, winding road known as Giant's Despair. Major General John Sullivan's 3,300 troops and 1,200 packhorses routed the Iroquois Confederation, destroying 40 of their towns.

Although both the Native Americans and the Yankees lost their jurisdiction of the area, the Connecticut migrants were allowed to keep their property and to remain as Pennsylvania residents.

Besides historical markers and an obelisk, a few sites hark back to the Valley's New England origins. West of the Susquehanna River in Wyoming stands the 1797 home of Luke Swetland, a settler who took care of the families hiding in the fort and was later captured by the Indians. His descendants held the house and its family heirlooms until 1958. Now the Wyoming Historical and Geological Society offers house tours, interpreting treasures of the 1830s.

In the borough of Forty Fort, near the point where Wyoming Avenue meets River Street, stands a meeting house built by the citizens for two congregations in 1807. The surrounding cemetery is the resting place of many of the area's first white settlers. A key figure was Nathan Denison, a colonel and county judge who took leadership in establishing this community of Yankees. His restored 1790 home is modeled after his grandfather's New England farmhouse. On three floors, the rooms radiate around a central chimney. Visitors enjoy seeing the bishop's chair, the seat favored by the bishop during his visits with the Denison family.

This house museum holds the distinction of being on a site high

ABOVE: *Among several monuments to the county's war dead on the lawn of Luzerne County Courthouse is a granite figure of an American combat soldier with a base engraved with the names of 83 Luzerne County men who died in the Vietnam War and seven who remain missing in action.*
RIGHT: *The Market Street Bridge is a distinguished and faithful landmark since it was built in 1929.*

enough to have avoided flooding, even during vicious Agnes in 1972. One cannot say the same for most of Wilkes-Barre, a city still girding its riverfront with levees. With a hint of its New England heritage in its name, the River Common stretches along the eastern shore of the Susquehanna from the Veterans Memorial Bridge at North Street to South Street. When it was named, the Common featured boat landings; it was the front porch view of Wilkes-Barre. Now downtown workers jog on the dike at lunchtime.

Ever since its completion in 1929, residents acclaim the Market Street Bridge as the city's gateway. Its limestone eagles, each 12 tons, set on pylons over the walkways at each end, are beloved talismans. Five lanes of traffic flow to and from Kingston on the west side. Each September, participants in the Riverside Rumble 10 K World Wheelchair Race barrel down the slope of the bridge to the finish line. Remarkably, this bridge held during each flood, and residents find security in its silhouette etched against the sky. The bridge leads to Public Square, a two-acre diamond at Market & Main Streets.

The square's diagonal design challenged architects designing buildings for the intersections. In the 1990s, the Greater Wilkes-Barre Chamber of Commerce restored what had been an 1895 five-story department store with a stunning corner entrance. The chamber stripped off the aluminum facade that had characterized Pomeroy's for 20th century shoppers and exposed beautiful arched windows set in stonework.

Five financial edifices in Wilkes-Barre's downtown rose in the early part of the 20th century and still stand. Their design was influenced by the City Beautiful Movement that grew out of Chicago's 1893 Columbian Exposition. The Mellon Bank Center at 8 West Market Street was designed by Chicago's Daniel H. Burnham, the main inspiration behind the Exposition.

With a plethora of renowned architects represent-ed in Wilkes-Barre, the city's Franklin Street boasts many outstanding structures. Who could overlook the four minarets of Irem Temple, a cultural venue built by the Irem Temple Shriners? St. Stephen's Episcopal Church, First United Methodist Church, and First Presbyterian Church, all late 19th century buildings, feature exteriors of local materials. The two buildings occupied by the Wyoming Historical and Geological Society Museum provide quiet research space surrounded by historic tomes and informative exhibits about the valley's past.

Don't miss the Osterhout Free Library just because it looks like a church! The structure was first a Presbyterian church by James Renwick, who designed St. Patrick's Cathedral in New York. The 1849 church was available when the estate of merchant Isaac S. Osterhout bequeathed money to establish a free library. Melvil Dewey, originator of the Dewey Decimal system of library book cataloging, arrived in Wilkes-Barre as a consultant and recommended that the church be adapted to use as a library so that the donation could be invested in books, etc. The first librarian was Hannah Packard James, a descendant of John Alden who came from Newton, Massachusetts. In 1889, she purchased almost 10,000 books and insisted that they be circulated. She planned what became one of the first children's rooms in an American library. In 1982, the area expanded to a children's wing.

Wilkes-Barre's economy has been spurred by efforts to restore properties for new uses. Builder Tom Murray, Sr., turned the three-block industrial site of Hazard Wireworks into a commercial complex. The boiler of this former manufacturer of cables became Murray's Inn, a restaurant-bar that attracts locals and out-of-towners.

After a two-decade fight to save this 65,000-square-foot red brick brewhouse built in the 1890s, the Stegmaier Brewery has been transformed into an award-winning federal office center. This facility,

Coal did matter here. By the 1870s, Wilkes-Barre's upper strata held success in anthracite and related industries so that their power extended throughout the northern coalfields. Their wealth grew from timberlands, utilities, transportation companies, banks, and insurance firms–and through marriages. Many elite homes rose in a downtown area that is today the River Street Historic District and includes more than 200 historic buildings.

Several South River Street buildings are now part of Wilkes University, a downtown liberal arts institution serving more than 3,000 students. Conyngham Hall at 130 and Chase Hall at 184 house administrative offices. At 146 South River Street the Annette Evans Alumni House is a Tudor Revival style structure that served as the home of Wilkes' first president.

The beautifully restored Kirby Hall at 202 is the former residence of Fred M. Kirby, who opened a five-and-ten-cent store in Wilkes-Barre about 1884 and expanded his F. M. Kirby and Company into a chain of 96 stores east of the Mississippi River. A 1912 merger made him a vice president of the new firm, F. W. Woolworth Company. A philanthropist in his beloved city, Kirby has his name attached to the Health Center on North Franklin Street. Its three floors are used by agencies to provide health-promoting services.

He also donated land along the western shore of the Susquehanna, now the city-owned Kirby Park of 111 acres. Each July 4, since America's bicentennial in 1976, crowds gather here to listen to the Northeastern Pennsylvania Philharmonic Orchestra mark Independence Day. Cannons boom and fireworks explode as the symphony plays the 1812 Overture. Created to bring the country into the city, Kirby Park is appreciated all summer for its mature oaks and maples shading grass that works as well for picnics as for cartwheels.

established by German immigrant Charles Stegmaier, is an outstanding Victorian industrial monument set off by a cupola.

Luzerne County Courthouse is at least as grand as it is artistic. In the springtime, cherry blossoms add to its year-round majesty. Laid out in the shape of a cruciform with its dome rising 100 feet above the first floor, the sandstone building went up in 1909 at a cost of $2 million.

The beauty of the interior is renowned. Mosaic backgrounds, marble columns, painted lunettes, and historical portraits decorate the vaulted ceilings and corridor decorations. Murals portray events in the history of Luzerne, from which four other counties–Susquehanna, Bradford, Lackawanna and Wyoming–were formed. There are also allegorical scenes that depict character traits and stained glass pictures that are realistic. One of the frescoes on the dome honors native George Catlin (1796-1872), who painted Native American customs. A panel in Courtroom No. 1 features a young Delaware maiden as a symbol of the Wyoming Valley, extending her hand to a coal miner with a mine entrance and a breaker in the background.

LEFT: *Italian tilework in the shape of a zodiac brightens the children's solarium room of the Kirby Health Center.*
RIGHT: *Symbolizing the area's ethnic traditions, the Polish Room in the Eugene S. Farley Library, Wilkes University, is a collection of artifacts and birch furnishings in the style of Zakopane, Poland.*

When the seasons change, and the symphony performs indoors, concert audiences flock to an Art Deco landmark on Public Square, the F. M. Kirby Center for the Performing Arts. In 1987, community leaders led by chain store president Al Boscov spearheaded the resurrection of this movie theater that had been state-of-the-art luxury in 1938. The Kirby Center presents an art film series, children's performances, and varied musical groups ranging from country to rock n' roll.

Each Thursday during the growing season, Wilkes-Barre's Public Square becomes a magnet for the business lunch crowd and the city's seniors. Well before noon food vendors start grilling hot dogs and stacking baked goods. But the biggest draw to the "farmer's market," as this event is called, is produce raised by Luzerne County farmers. Harold Golomb stacks sweet corn in August and squash in October. Unassuming but observant, he mentions that he has been hauling vegetables and flowers from his 40-acre farm in Plains since the market opened "before Agnes, the flood." A charter member, he adheres to the county's policy, "You must grow it to sell it." His son calls over for another basket of eggplants. His wife explains how hot the peppers are.

In another part of the Square, I catch a whiff of the aroma of deep-blue Concord grapes, a short-lived early autumn scent. A nearby table holds various fruits, all from Brace's Orchard near Dallas. Their 150-acre farm has been in the Brace family for seven generations, more than a century. From their 80 acres of apples, they press and pasteurize their own cider as well as pick fruit for direct sale. As Nancy Brace points out Ginger Gold, a crisp yellow apple propagated from five different apples, she describes with in-house delight how the Braces test a new strain of fruit, offering a sampling to their customers and planting more trees if the response is favorable.

There is forthrightness in the approach of these farmers and in the zeal and pluck with which the residents of Wilkes-Barre have built their city and rebuilt it when necessary. Creative change may not come quickly, but when it does, it comes with a no-nonsense approach. Their immigrant heritage holds sway with plenty of stamina. Here Planters Peanuts originated and the cartoon character Joe Palooka was born. No one overlooks the fact that the city's namesakes, John Wilkes and Isaac Barre, upheld colonial independence in English Parliament, or that the earliest European settlers fought earnestly for the Wyoming Valley.

RIGHT: *Luzerne County Courthouse, an 1897 Renaissance-style edifice, stands in a landscaped park typical of civic buildings that were built during the "White Cities Movement."* **BELOW:** *Inside the courthouse, mosaic tiles and allegorical lunette oil paintings decorate the ceilings of the East Wing corridor surrounding the rotunda. The oval portraits are of John Franklin, a prominent early citizen, and Nathan Dennison, a soldier and judge.*

LEFT: *Currently a women's residence hall, Weiss Hall (1850) at 98 South River Street, is a turreted, richly textured Queen Anne-style house that was donated to Wilkes University in 1957 by Mr. and Mrs. Aaron Weiss.* **BELOW:** *The Eleanor Farley Room at Wilkes University honors the wife of the institution's first president, a woman of warmth who entertained students and valued the fine arts.*

BELOW: *In the design of a bursting sun, the stained glass dome in the auditorium of Temple Israel, 237 South River Street, rises 42 feet above the floor.*
RIGHT: *Built in honor of Angeline Elizabeth Kirby (1832-1932), the Kirby Memorial Health Center, 71 North Franklin Street, houses health services and organizations. The lobby, decorated with an English oak ceiling and hand-fired tiles with Moorish motifs, features a bronze wall sculpture of Mrs. Kirby as a grandmother and an oil painting of Florence Nightingale by Abraham Solomon (1824-1862).*

RIGHT: *A terra cotta detail enlivens the Art Deco exterior of the F.M. Kirby Center for the Performing Arts. (1937)* FAR RIGHT: *The Purin Bulgarian National Folk Ensemble performs on the stage of the F.M. Kirby Center for the Performing Arts.* BELOW RIGHT: *The restored Kirby Center and the 14-story PNC Bank Building (1928) straddle the southeast quadrant of the diamond called Public Square.* BELOW: *These lights beckon patrons of all tastes to evening performances at the former Paramount and earlier Comerford Movie Theater.*

ABOVE: *"In front of the Westmoreland Club, springtime" could be the caption of the photo being taken here at the exclusive club on Franklin Street.* **TOP RIGHT:** *This bird's-eye view of Wilkes-Barre and the Market Street Bridge spanning the flood-prone Susquehanna, presents downtown structures surrounding Public Square.* **BELOW RIGHT:** *Spring arrives at River Common near the campus of King's College.*

LEFT: *Memorable for its four towering minarets, the Irem Temple was completed by its Shriners in 1908, patterning the interior after St. Sophia's Mosque in Constantinople.* RIGHT: *Stained glass gleams in the ceiling of the auditorium of the Irem Temple on North Franklin Street.* BELOW: *With a Gothic bell tower outside and a quality organ inside, St. Stephen's Episcopal Church on South Franklin Street has served its congregation and the downtown community since it was built of local stone in 1896.*

BELOW: *Public Square becomes a farmers' market and lunchtime mecca during the growing season. From their farm near Plains, the Golomb family has hauled produce each week since the '70s.* **TOP RIGHT:** *Now a Federal office building and nationally recognized for its restoration as an industrial complex, the Stegmaier Brewing Company was the third largest brewery in Pennsylvania in 1974. The brewhouse was built in the 1890s.* **BELOW RIGHT:** *Flush with Victorian details, Wilkes-Barre City Hall (1893) is the city's first and only municipal hall.*

COUNTY SEATS AND OTHER MEMORABLE PLACES

The locations of regional towns often are rooted in their geography or the needs of early settlers. There are river towns such as Milford along the Delaware in Pike County and White Haven beside the Lehigh in Luzerne County. Places such as Tunkhannock, Wyalusing, Tamaqua, and Shawnee-on-the-Delaware were either towns or trail sites of the Lenapes, called Delawares by European settlers. Towns such as Susquehanna, Honesdale, and Carbondale thrived as rail centers.

Stroudsburg, the urban center of the Poconos and the seat of Monroe County, flourished historically in several regards. The hotel at 700 Main Street was a stop on the stagecoach route from Easton to Milford. Also, the borough and East Stroudsburg, its sister across Brodhead Creek, had stations for two rail lines. From 1900, tourists traveled the "Phoebe Snow" to reach their resort destinations in the Poconos. Today, dining and shopping for railroad momentos goes on at the restored Dansbury Depot.

During a walking tour, I noted several structures that harked back to early commerce. Here J. J. Newberry opened the first of a chain of department stores sprinkled throughout the East Coast after the 1930s. That entrepreneurial spirit is alive in the businesses that front Main and several other streets. A cyber café and a bagel shop have joined florists and insurance agencies. Eateries benefit from student consumers at East Stroudsburg University on the hill.

In Pennsylvania's northeast, a commons or central green provides a setting in which to showcase the courthouse. This influence arrived with early settlers from New England. The space in front of the Monroe County Courthouse is very abbreviated compared to the spacious square surrounding the courthouse in LaPorte (Sullivan County). Vivian McCarty, Sullivan's first elected female commissioner, initiated the building of a gazebo for performers in the square across the street from the courthouse.

In Montrose "the green" separates the Susquehanna County Courthouse from the library and firehouse. The blueberry festival during the first week of August lures a crowd to the green. An arts and crafts show in the same location is even more popular. All year, residents of this county seat take pride in its sizable number of restored stately homes. Many are white frame structures with green shutters.

Tunkhannock is a county seat that does not hide its village-like nature. There is a rural ideal in the neat, residential streets with the Susquehanna River flowing on the outskirts. Farms and mountains nudge quite close to the town's lifeline, the intersection of U.S. Route 6 (Scranton-Towanda) and U.S. Route 29 (Wilkes-Barre-Binghamton). Riverside Park was developed in the 1990s, and nearby, scenic Lake Carey slowly recovers from a brutal tornado. The centerpiece is the Wyoming County Courthouse, but there's a sense that life percolating in other parts of this level town is just as important.

Farther south, Pottsville's courthouse maintains a hilltop position. In fact, the main attractions of this county seat of Schuylkill have never hid behind a bushel. Who could miss the statue of Henry Clay towering on a pedestal at the southern end of Pottsville since 1855? Why feature a sculpture of someone who never set foot here? Clay's protective tariffs paved the way for an economic boom here in the

ABOVE: *Dusk brings on commercial lights of a thriving Main Street in Stroudsburg, Monroe's county seat and an urban axis in the Poconos.*
RIGHT: *Lehighton Band, a marching and concert band since 1864, plays a July "Concert Under the Stars" in the borough's park, Carbon County.*

southern anthracite field before the Civil War, and in gratitude, Pottsville's coal barons honored the Kentucky senator with this lofty sculpture soon after his death.

Nearby, both Mahantongo and Norwegian Streets are hills to reckon with. On the first stands America's oldest brewery, where the Yuengling family has been making beer for five generations. As a college freshman, I "adult-sat" the matriarch of this family each Sunday night when her wait staff was off duty. I viewed her English Tudor home and gardens as an art piece and appreciate that as the current home of the Schuylkill County Council for the Arts, more people can enjoy the fine wood paneling and stained glass of the Frank D. Yuengling Mansion.

So many of the settlements that grew on the backs of anthracite industries still have churches that reflect the specific heritage of immigrants. In Schuylkill County's Frackville, Lackawanna County's Olyphant and Luzerne County's White Haven, religious structures are prominent. Welsh, Baptist, Ukrainian Catholic, Russian Orthodox and Polish Catholic churches are only a few of many in Plymouth, Edwardsville, Kingston, and Forty Fort, a string of boroughs along U.S. Route 11. Hawley, at the edge of Lake Wallenpaupak, boasts a Church Street with five churches within two blocks.

The Northeast can brag of dozens of boroughs with a distinctive district, a quaint downtown, or a featured attraction. Each holds a story about its past. Most hold locally-sponsored events.

One July evening, I found a wooden seat in front of the bandshell in Lehighton's central park. The Lehighton Band, with origins going back to 1864, played some Sousa numbers and other marches. While kids caught fireflies, and toddlers did gymnastics on a metal railing, the rest of the audience–mostly seniors–listened from semi-circular rows set on a grade. Commenting on the less- than-thriving

business district below the bandshell, one old-timer remembered that, "Thirty years ago there were so many people shopping Friday nights that you couldn't cross First Street." This Carbon County town exudes nostalgia.

A longing for the past also rises when one *happens* upon the borough of Weatherly in Carbon County. A curve in the road, a bridge over Black Creek and then a quaint railroad station serving as the borough offices leads to the valley floor of Weatherly with dwellings on two hillsides. Most prominent is a clock tower atop the three-story Weatherly School, built by Charles Schwab, a president of Bethlehem Steel who gave the building to the town where his wife, Eurana Dinkey, was born. In 1913 she presented a park with a playground and bandshell to Weatherly.

Honesdale was once a key transportation hub, launching America's first million-dollar enterprise, the Delaware & Hudson Canal. It teamed with a gravity railroad in the early 1800s to ship hundreds of tons of coal each day from the mines of Carbondale to Roundout, New York. For a stretch of time, Honesdale was the largest coal storage center in the world.

Native Tom Fasshauer prizes his town's heritage and appreciates the downtown museum at the Wayne County Historical Society that does the same. He also values its quality of life. "Honesdale is laid out nicely with downtown events and flourishing businesses. It is a family town within a region offering safe schools." Fasshauer's family retail business occupies a 150-year-old structure on Main Street.

The Route 6 entrance into Hawley passes Bingham Park, an outdoor sports center conserving a natural community setting. In well-designed diamonds, courts, and fields, kids and families play team sports. Their summer excitement was infectious as I watched from my upper room in the Settlers Inn across the street. I strolled to the edge of the inn's

lawn beyond a secluded mini-beach along the Lackawaxen River. A warbler sang and a fly fisher waded downriver for a few more casts before dusk.

Main Avenue makes this Victorian-style borough a take-notice place. Antique shops, delis, and printers are among its commercial enterprises. The Falls Port Inn and Restaurant that Baron von Eckleburg created on the corner at 330 Main Avenue in 1902 is again serving hungry and tired guests. Another distinctive structure is the Ritz Company Playhouse with its Art Deco style marquee. Two buildings of native bluestone–a former glass works and a silk mill–now cater to tourists by selling antiques and providing lodging.

The town of Milford possessed sophistication in the late 19th century in two regards–as a summer resort and a commercial crossroads. Prosperous entrepreneurs e.g., the Pinchots, chose this eastern site on the Delaware River to build very comfortable summer homes. Artists influenced by the Hudson River School interfaced with commercially minded settlers developing the area with pride. A walking tour guide of this well-planned borough underscores the architectural quality of its buildings today. The historic district is in the town center with Broad Street at its heart. Along that street in a splendid structure housing the Pike County Historical Society is Hiawatha, a stage coach that brought vacationers to the west side of the Delaware River. In that era the river was seasonally "fordable" at Milford. At least seven mills served the area in the 1800s.

Perhaps the town's name evolved from these two realities.

It is a worthwhile venture to see the restored Upper Mill with a working water wheel on Sawkill Creek. Circa 1882, it was the Jervis Gordon Grist Mill. Shops in the complex demonstrate the ingenuity of historically-minded residents such as Bob Hartman, one of the mill's three restorers. Such preservation endeavors beckon residents to Pennsylvania boroughs and their surrounding townships.

Some residents strategize carefully to live year-round in the scenic countryside that they once enjoyed only on vacation. Eva Olszewski found it harder and harder to return to New Jersey's congestion after weekends in the Endless Mountains. When she could not find a job as a chemist in Bradford County, she left her profession and learned baking to fill a product need in Stevensville. In 1995, she built and cured a brick oven. Customers from as far east as Allentown and as far

ABOVE: *Known as "The Columns," and now home of the Pike County Historical Society, this neoclassic former summer home (1904-1907) has 24 rooms.*

TOP RIGHT: *Atop First Presbyterian Church (1874) is Milford's "town clock," donated in 1887 by William Bross, the first signer of the constitutional amendment abolishing slavery.*

west as Wellsboro buy her baked goods at the Apple Tree Bakery.

Fuel for the Stevensville oven is hardwood scraps from local sawmills. Other northeast companies rely on local natural resources for their production. Employees at Bradford Basket Company in Troy hand-weave red maple strips into beautiful baskets. Larrmer & Norton turns white ash lumber into blanks that become baseball bats. Cherry and maple lumber becomes fine furniture. In Stevensville, Dotti-Lou Meats processes deer into kielbassi and jerky for hundreds of hunters. Endless Mountain Stone Company in Susquehanna County quarries bluestone rock for patios and lawn ornaments, and sugar shacks in several counties boil maple sap into syrup and other sweet products. For example, in Warren Center (Bradford Co.), the Dewing family prepares maple sugar items for gift packets.

But a prime focus of the workers of this region is serving tourists. In the summer, Pike County's head count grows five times to 200,000 people. These vacationers hike to cascades, go antiquing in historic towns, and canoe down the Delaware River. When weekenders cannot bear to leave, they start considering being based in a picturesque Pennsyvania setting and gleaning satisfaction from a more relaxed lifestyle.

LEFT: *Rich with such details as a mansard roof, a domed cupola, and arched Palladian windows, the Pike County Courthouse (1874) serves this mushrooming area from Broad Street in Milford.*
NEXT PAGES: *Dallas Senior High School flag twirlers march in Hazleton's Funfest parade, the climax of the September street fair that draws thousands of area residents to Broad Street (Luzerne County).*

HAZLETON'S CAN DO

We went straight to the city's lifeblood on my tour of Hazleton with Joe Yenchko. This native of Pennsylvania's highest city took me beyond the residential section–streets named for trees and presidents and lined with small bungalows covered with siding. We crossed Route 924 and entered a spaciously developed industrial park called Valmont. The sight of corporate signage and factories that this retired community developer knows well set his tongue loose. "These are income-producing monuments built on strip mine areas that we reclaimed." The "we" that this energetic man is talking about is CAN DO, a public, non-profit corporation that saved the Hazleton area from anthracite bankruptcy. Working since 1956, CAN DO brought in more than 100 diversified companies, which created about 10,000 jobs and constructed 147 buildings. It all began with the concern of locals.

In the 1950s, when flooding from a hurricane dealt a death blow to the waning coal industry, a core of Chamber of Commerce members stopped wringing their hands and put their heads to work. With Dr. Edgar Dessen, a radiologist in the lead, CAN DO garnered 100 per cent community support for their dime-a-week fund drive. To buy land for industrial development, there were bigger fund drives, time-consuming recruitment, and the building of factory shells and utility systems.

Our tour went back and forth across Valmont's 835 acres. Yenchko proudly mentioned the products that were being manufactured in the structures in front of my eyes: "All Steel Corporation–steel office furniture; International Paper Corporation–phone book covers; Dial Corporation–soap and household cleaners; Stroehman Bakeries baking 10,000 loaves of bread per hour."

When we passed the neatly landscaped property of General Foam Corporation, which makes polyurethane products, Yenchko explained, "This is the first company we brought in, and they've expanded seven times." CAN DO adhered to a winning formula–a 60,000 square foot factory employing 100 people to be put up on each ten acres of land. CAN DO has acquired 4,000 acres of land divided into five industrial parks.

The persistence of dozens of volunteers kept up the momentum of attracting companies and smoothing frustrating snags. Several key players worked relentlessly in the CAN DO headquarters in the Markle Building. Dessen was like a beam of light in every negotiation with a prospective company. Attorney Lou Feldman and CPA Joe Weber ingeniously put together financial alternatives while architect John DePierro showed up at a moment's notice to discuss factory design. Joe Yenchko learned from authorities in planning how to build and maintain industrial parks. Each of these natives had a strong work ethic. In the background of one, Joe Yenchko, is an immigrant story that mirrors that of many coal crackers.

In 1910, George Yenchko left his peasant strivings and a young bride in Slovakia to carve out a better life in America. Able-bodied from working the land, this young Slav got off the ship in New York and found work in the anthracite mines of northeastern Pennsylvania. Two years later, his wife Mary and their toddler traveled by horse-cart to catch a freighter to make the same transatlantic journey. Mary's arrival and George's employment qualified them for company housing in a tarpaper dwelling in the patch town of Humboldt.

Over their years in Luzerne County they worked hard, raising eight children. Gradually but steadily George improved their situation by going down into the mines every day possible and banking his wages of each optional day. These savings enabled the family to buy their own small double house, live on one side and pay the mortgage with the rent from the other half. Squeezing out from the financial thumb of the mining company, they put roots down in Hazleton, a settlement that mushroomed into a city with the coal industry. For 33 years, George worked underground without seeing sunlight, dreaming that his six sons and two daughters would have a better workday.

Sending them to high school was part of his strategy. But economic downturn continued with coal production decreasing. When his son Joe graduated from Hazleton City High in 1937, 65 percent of the 450 graduates planned to leave the area. Some did so to serve during World War II. Several veterans in the Yenchko family surprisingly returned to Hazleton. Joe and his three brothers utilized their mechanical aptitude and formed a plumbing and heating company to meet the post-war demand for indoor plumbing and central heating systems.

They had work, but with the economic situation worsening in the fifties, they saw that there would be no work for their children. For example, 128 families migrated to Rochester, New York, for employment. The situation prompted Joe Yenchko to get involved with CAN DO. In this spirit, he reinvested in the Hazleton area just as his father George had poured his energy into mining the Middle Coal Field. These two generations of men made a difference in the place they claimed as home for their families.

LEFT: *Joseph Yenchko (left), a Hazleton native who worked for CAN DO first as a volunteer business owner and then until 1984 as executive director, chats with current president W. Kevin O'Donnell in front of the city's CAN DO building, where job creation has gone on successfully since the 1950s.* **ABOVE LEFT:** *In coal-mining communities, Catholic dioceses established schools and hospitals such as St. Joseph's in Hazleton. This is the original entrance of the present expanded medical center.* **ABOVE RIGHT:** *Hazleton's Laurel Street retains the mansions of former coal barons and investors. This many-featured dwelling at 219 North Laurel was built by banker William Lawall.*

LEFT: *Spurred by the Delaware and Hudson Canal Company, Honesdale was named after Philip Hone, a president of that company. The Wayne County Courthouse has been situated in Honesdale since it became the county seat in 1842.* **BELOW**: *The corner in Hawley where Church Street intersects with Main Avenue (U.S. Route 6) was vital since the turn of the 20th century when Baron von Eckelberg opened an inn in this scenic borough, then called Falls Port, Wayne County.* **BOTTOM**: *Honesdale's Main Street provides the businesses vital to a small but prospering community of more than 5,000 residents.*

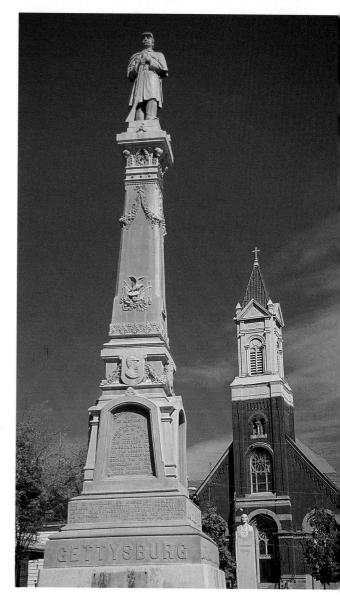

ABOVE: *Constructed of sandstone in 1891, the Schuylkill County Courthouse towers high in Pottsville, the county seat.* **LEFT**: *From Carbondale's central plaza rises war monuments and, at the end, the spire of St. Rose of Lima Church (Lackawanna County).* **FAR LEFT**: *Today, Sonestown is a lodging stop for travelers on Route 220 just as it was in the late 1800s. North of this Sullivan County village spreads the awe-inspiring Endless Mountains. TOP LEFT*: *Carbondale's Victorian-style homes were constructed when anthracite was king (Lackawanna County).* **NEXT PAGES**: *Built by Jacob Stroud (1735-1806), the founder of Stroudsburg, the Stroud Mansion, 900 Main Street, was the residence of Jacob's son Daniel, a Quaker who was instrumental in laying out the borough's streets. Local history unfolds during a tour of the mansion, now home to the Monroe County Historical Society.*

LEFT: *The clock in Eagles Mere symbolizes this charming Sullivan County settlement, a long-time draw for vacationers.* **BELOW:** *Bradford's county seat, Towanda, lies along the bank of the north branch of the Susquehanna River. The dome of the sandstone courthouse (1898) rises in the downtown.* **BELOW RIGHT:** *Located one block from U.S. Route 6 in Tunkhannock, the Wyoming County Courthouse is a fine example of Italianate architecture. Built in 1843, it was enlarged in 1869 and 1992.*

JIM THORPE, A RESTORED TOURIST TOWN

Power concentrated here in the 19th century as America's rising industrial leaders built homes in Mauch Chunk. In the 1870s, 13 of America's 26 millionaires lived here in this deep-cut valley town. Their residences of striking architectural styles now line the Historic District as shops and B&Bs.

One of the most lavish mansions is open to the public. Touring the hilltop home of coal and railroad entrepreneur Asa Packer reveals one of the nation's most perfectly preserved Italian villas. From Jim Thorpe's Sunrise Diner, where the rice pudding is unparalleled, I skirted the Carbon County Courthouse and climbed to the wide porch of the 1860 mansion. Inside, the ornate furnishings are the same as they were in 1878 for Packers' 50th wedding anniversary party. Among the 1,000 guests for the big event were the Rockefellers and the Wanamakers. Guests may have noticed the peacock table, an 1865 gift from Queen Victoria, or the crystal chandelier that was later copied for the set of "Gone With the Wind." Redecorating included hiring 16 European artisans to carve 1,500 flower motifs–each distinctive–for the woodwork. The textured design on the dining room walls was done by

ABOVE: *Jim Thorpe's Broad Street boasts of restored Victorian-style dwellings, now residences and shops that invite tourists.* **RIGHT:** *Unique businesses and architectural details woo visitors to enjoy Jim Thorpe, former coal town of Mauch Chunk, on foot.* **TOP RIGHT:** *Diners enjoy this antique-laden setting at Sequoyah House, a restaurant that serves a gourmet, health-conscious menu.*

pressing 24-karat gold overlay on stenciled gravel. Today I listen to a full-bodied tune played by a Welty Cottage orchestrion, which includes 62 pipes and several percussion instruments.

The tour of this treasure-filled home informs me that Asa Packer was as generous as he was wealthy. Packer donated the property and a $500,000 endowment for the 1866 opening of Lehigh University in South Bethlehem. In total, Packer, who had the equivalent of an eighth grade education, provided more than $3 million and offered leadership for what is today an esteemed educational institution. Beloved by his employees and associates, Packer acted with humility and kindness. He paid his employees of the Lehigh Valley Railroad while they were serving in the Civil War. Residents mourned his death and approved of a Puck cartoon that depicted Packer as a philanthropist liberally scattering money to charities in the manner that Johnny Appleseed tossed seeds to plant trees.

To see an example of the Packers' benevolence towards religious institutions, I crossed Asa Packer Park opposite the railroad station, a source for tourist information, and hiked up Race Street to tour St. Mark's Episcopal Church. A cast iron elevator takes parishioners to the sanctuary with its notable art treasures. The reredos of Caen stone and the altar of exquisite marble memorialize Packer's life. In the

afternoon sun the Louis Tiffany windows gleam with brilliance. Lit gas standards turn the baptismal font into a vivid art piece.

The borough's Victoriana is most appreciated by staying in one of the B&Bs on Broadway such as The Victoriann, where the decor helps you relive the late 1800s. A ride on the train and visits to the museum and the jail keep you learning about the period.

The Old Jail Museum is a former prison, built in 1871. Its underground cells become more eerie as a tour guide relates that several Molly Maguires, who were of Irish descent, were hanged in this prison in the late 1870's following a rash of labor violence. Controversial trials resulted in the conviction and death of 20 men, some in this Carbon County Jail. Don't miss the handprint in cell 17, a mysterious image supposedly remaining as one Molly Maguire's claim to innocence.

ABOVE: *The dining room in the Asa Packer Mansion (1860) in Jim Thorpe illustrates the wealth of this coal and railroad industrialist/philanthropist. The furnishings, all from the Packers, make up one of America's finest post-Civil War collections in a private dwelling.* **RIGHT:** *Visitors tour St. Mark's Episcopal Church on Race Street and enjoy its Tiffany stained glass and Caen stonework and other religious art pieces donated by the Packers.*

Tourists flocked here in the late 1800s to "do the Switchback, America's first tourist railroad." The Mauch Chunk Museum exhibits the ads that drew rail excursionists from as far away as New York and Baltimore to ride a train on a route that was used earlier to haul coal from the mines at Summit Hill to the edge of the Lehigh River. Most fascinating is the museum's working model of this attraction as it operated in 1895, taking up to 10,000 people up the mountain for the "Grand View" and then coasting down Mt. Jefferson, perhaps with a stop for a picnic or swim. The Switchback Railroad declined as did mining and the whole economy of Carbon County. Besides, the lovely town was periodically inundated when the Mauch Chunk Creek overflowed.

In the 1950s, locals began recovery efforts with a "nickel-a-week" campaign to revitalize the economy. Simultaneously, the widow of Jim Thorpe, an athlete with Native American heritage, made a deal with the town so they would name it after her husband and bury him there, memorializing him with a tombstone, all with publicity focused on increasing the fund. Articles by Joe Boyle, a civic-minded journalist in the borough, reached far and wide, and efforts by Agnes McCartney created Mauch Chunk Lake, which stopped the flooding and provided a water supply with recreational benefits. Area

residents flock to the beach and visitors camp at this Carbon County park. The work of so many folks over the years resulted in a renaissance for Jim Thorpe that has brought businesses and tourists.

Gains in economic growth hark back to the many tourists who head for whitewater recreation on the Lehigh or for biking on the rail trail of the Delaware & Lehigh National Heritage Corridor. This is to the liking of Paul Fogal, a New Jersey import whose family company, Pocono Whitewater Ltd., offers guided rafting, kayaking, hiking, or biking. On mountain bikes or hybrids, the ride through the gorge goes gently downhill for 25 miles on a converted railroad bed with a stop at the picturesque Glen Onoko Falls.

Wearing jeans and biking to work, this tall, lean man is an experienced paddler on three continents and appreciates how quickly the Lehigh can change its mood. In 1999, for example, the river was at its lowest level, 56 cubic feet per second, on a Tuesday. Two days later Hurricane Floyd had swollen the river to a raging 3,000 c.f.s. Past entrepreneurs harnessed the river's power to ship coal via a series of locks.

Today the water release program by the U.S. Army Corps of Engineers controls the water level for season-long recreation. This exciting river and its historic surroundings entice visitors to a topnotch stay in Jim Thorpe.

UNFORGETTABLE ATTRACTIONS IN THE REGION

Photo: Pocono Raceway

It draws the biggest crowd in the Northeast. Two weekends out of the year during NASCAR events, the Pocono Raceway becomes a city, its population just under that of Philadelphia or Pittsburgh. Tens of thousands of fans take Exit 43 from I-80 to watch their favorite race team zoom around the track at well over 200 mph on Sunday afternoon.

But the hype begins much earlier, on Thursday. Fans crowd at I-81 overpasses to get a glimpse of the tractor trailer transporter carrying their favorite car. On the truck is painted a mural of the car inside as well as its driver and his autograph in a 20-foot scrawl. For instance, a car sponsored by General Mills will be yellow and blue, the colors of the Cheerios box.

Loyalty is hefty and growing for these American drivers racing in hand-built American cars. In the '90s, Pennsylvania's governor declared Exit 43 the Richard Petty Exit, naming it for a retired race winner whose number was also 43. In keeping with a national sports trend, on two summer weekends, 1,300 acres of the pristine Poconos come under the spell of NASCAR Winston Cup racing fans.

At NASCAR it's speed that lures the fans; at Steamtown NHS, it's power that moves weight. I felt dwarfed by the locomotives in Steamtown's repair shop. A crane was lifting a 5-ton wheel. Local railroad aficionados were working as volunteers on the restoration of the former Pennsylvania Railroad's K-4 locomotive No. 1361, which was built in 1918. Lathes, milling machines and various machine tools facilitate rebuilding worn parts for locomotives that weigh more than 400,000 pounds. Heavy metal, indeed.

Because steam locomotives require more maintenance than diesel engines, there is a lot to do in this "big garage." One mechanic had climbed down into the inspection pit to clean out the firebox of No. 3254. Burning coal must exceed 2,000 degrees F. to turn the water in the boiler to steam. The boiler must be checked for cracks and new tubes installed

periodically. Besides the locomotive repair shop, there were many other fascinations at this 40-acre attraction, the only place in North America where you can experience the steam railroad in full context.

From this former hub of the Delaware, Lackawanna and Western Railroad, I enjoyed riding one of Steamtown's excursion trains to Moscow. As our steam-billowing locomotive pulled out of the station, our car host, Bill Nalavanko, pointed out the former shops of the D L & W, now a government-owned artillery factory. The train passed north of the Scranton Iron Furnaces, where iron was smelted for T-rail production. Also, America's first steel rails were manufactured at these furnaces and placed Scranton at the top of the industrial revolution.

Our route went through the Nay Aug tunnel with Bill warning us to keep the windows closed so that the cinders from the smokestack did not blow in on our clothes. The tracks went alongside Roaring Brook. Because it was too chilly for sunbathing, the rock at a scenic pool known among area college students as Bare Ass Beach was indeed bare. The view opened up as we passed two Scranton reservoirs, No. 7 and No. 9. Going uphill, our top speed was 29 mph. After a stop at Moscow, we returned, again passing mossy walls oozing with springs and scenic views. One exception was a huge vehicle graveyard, the site of one of the world's largest auto recyclers. As we approached Scranton,

ABOVE: *NASCAR Winston Cup races swell the Pocono Raceway's population beyond 100,000, creating the third largest city in Pennsylvania.* **RIGHT:** *Illusionists Dorothy Dietrich and John Bravo offer visitors to Houdini Museum in Scranton insight into the magic and stuntwork of the famed Harry Houdini (1874-1926), who performed in the city.*

Bill noted that the former Lackawanna Station, a magnificent French Renaissance-style structure, is now a hotel.

Also in view was the Lackawanna County Trolley Museum, a 1999 structure with exhibits on the era of trolleys. In 1886, Scranton launched the first successful electrified trolley system in America, and it ran continuously until 1954. It occurred to me that another excursion, this one in a trolley, would be a good idea in Scranton, the Electric City. Alighting, I gazed in amazement at the enormous locomotive that had just pulled our car, an "iron horse."

Real horses bring another kind of enjoyment to the northeast. Fans of live harness racing light on Pocono Downs near Wilkes-Barre several nights a week between April and November. By post time, fans have wagered on the standardbreds that they feel will be "in the money." For each race, up to eight horses trot to their positions and then explode from the gate, gaining a top speed of 35 mph. On the track between the ages of two and 14, a horse usually races once a week.

On summer evenings it is great to take it all in at trackside or from the grandstand. Some serious horseplayers gravitate to the Sports Bar. The Pacers Clubhouse features a panoramic view of the track with a varied menu. Each table has its own television monitor, with several equipped with self-betting terminals. Regulars use their Tiny Tim, a computerized account, to wager on live and simulcast races year-round.

Exit 46 off I-81 zips to a another year-round venue, First Union Arena at Casey Plaza. At the Arena, a $44 million facility, ice hockey fans attend the Wilkes-Barre/Scranton Penguins home games. Collegiate sports events include basketball. Trade shows, nationally-known concert artists, and graduation ceremonies are only a few of the events that this versatile setting hosts. The Arena attracts

patrons from the 13.6 million residents within a 100-mile radius.

Why shouldn't the Houdini Museum look like an ordinary row house in Scranton? After all, its namesake liked bringing magic to the commonplace. Born as Erich Weiss, Houdini became a world-renowned illusionist and escape artist. His remarkable feats, skillfully presented around the globe, have made his name a metaphor, e.g., That clever guy pulled a houdini!

In the 1920s, Houdini drew a full house at the Poli, a Scranton vaudeville theater in the 200 block of Wyoming Avenue. Now much smaller and renamed the Ritz, Poli's in its heyday held 2,000 people, and when Houdini was billed, was filled to capacity six days a week. Here Houdini escaped from a barrel of beer, leaving it intact and full. His skills and winning manner thrilled his audiences.

Today, students and families head to this attraction on North Main Street in Scranton for an award-winning show. The museum tour reveals much about Houdini's life and features acts by two famed magicians, John Bravo and Dorothy Dietrich. Called the female Houdini, Dietrich does mystifying feats and disappearing acts similar to those Houdini did. Children leave with a new magic trick up their sleeves!

Children also learn–in this setting as participants– at Quiet Valley Living Historical Farm south of Stroudsburg. During the "Schoolhouse Experience," for instance, children in a one-room school of the past do slate assignments and recitations, have a spelling bee, and play old-time games. During the school year, more than 12,000 children from area schools learn about history by reliving it.

But Quiet Valley produces far more than scholars. This 114-acre property, now a private, non-profit corporation, functions to show how four generations lived together, worked together, and played together– making a good life. Quiet Valley focuses on recreating farm life as it was in 1830. At that time the family was fond of rye and vegetables and raised flax, processing, dyeing, and weaving it into clothing. Smoking meat, drying fruits, and baking bread are a few of the many necessary tasks performed by volunteers to keep food on the table.

When I arrived, I slowed my car on the dirt lane so that a gaggle of geese could proceed. Guinea fowl ran en flock and roosters strutted near a thriving hen house. (I learned later that one staff member incubates eggs in her bathroom to show visiting schoolchildren how chicks hatch.) Molly, the dark

sheep, is the focus of attention during a lesson on wool-processing. The breeds of the farm animals could have been at Quiet Valley in the 19th century.

While the Belgian workhorses and a short-horned

cow grazed in the meadow, I went inside the farmhouse to find out more about daily life here. Surprisingly, a spry, elderly woman in a nightgown rolled out of bed and popped out from behind the bed curtain. She introduced herself as a midwife, explaining that she was sleeping late because she had been up all night delivering a baby. She believes in having a large family because "young 'uns is for work." She feels that women don't need to know how to read or write–"if you got a good man." Then she looks for support among the men in the audience, "Isn't that right?"

More than beliefs have been held over from the 19th century on this farm. When Alice and Wendell Wicks bought this property in 1958, it was functioning in a bygone era. Left with the belongings of several generations, the Wicks realized that their purchase was too unique to carve into building lots. After offering slice-of-history parties to their friends, the Wicks felt that this treasure should be available for the public to know the ways of pioneer farmers who worked hard to thrive.

The Wicks' daughter Sue and her husband Gary Oiler joined them to develop a year-round educational program. The farm is open to the public from June 20 to Labor Day so that visitors can learn about America's past. Quiet Valley guides dress and speak as country people did in the early 19th century. With the animals and crops to tend, there's not much time for the parlor, "a room that is just for setting."

Farther north in New Milford's Old Mill Village

Museum, people portray the heritage of settlers in the Endless Mountains. On summer Sundays one can observe blacksmithing, quilting, and other life skills essential in the 1800s.

Even though the winters of northeast Pennsylvania can be brutal, residents gain helpful guidance on Zone 5 gardening at Greystone Gardens. Its English-born owner, Paul Epsom, sells shrubs and perennials that tolerate a long, freezing winter that may begin October 15.

Many northeasterners learn Epsom's humor-laced gardening tips on his WNEP-TV show, but it is more intriguing to go to the gardens in person, if only to take a spot of tea on the Café's veranda. I approached the property situated in a hollow along U.S. Routes 6/11 north of Clarks Summit. With Harry, an Irish terrier, at his heels, Epsom gave me a tour of several landscaped micro-climates. In the woodland garden, he pointed out a stunning red shrub aronia arbifolia, a witch hazel, and ground cover phlox. In the dry micro-climate grew ornamental goldenrod and an Eastern red cedar. Plant stock comes from northern sources in New York and Minnesota to ensure its resilience to survive winter.

To prevent deer destruction of plantings, a common discouragement to suburbanites, Epsom recommends plant species and garden designs that deter these browsers. I observed healthy groups of spireas, hostas, and sedums. I enjoyed strolling through the display gardens where everything was identified. Points of interest such as ponds, trellises, gateways, and bird feeders enhanced this bright plant environment. In this attractive setting and in the presence of this fun-loving Brit, I got enthusiastic about planting.

Ten miles north of Scranton, the Vileniki Herb Farm offers 400 varieties of herbs, fresh and dried. Classes educate patrons on the plants' culinary, medicinal, and ornamental purposes. Owner Gerry Janus named the enterprise after "eastern wood

ABOVE: Observing plants in a landscaped environment educates customers at Greystone Gardens near Clarks Summit, Lackawanna County. RIGHT: The Pacer's Clubhouse at Pocono Downs offers tableside betting, serves entrees, and a view of live harness horse racing.

spirits who taught earthlings how to benefit from the healing qualities of herbs." Workshops teach how to make herbal gifts and how to preserve fresh herbs. Gift shop customers often attend the farm's events, e.g., a weekly tea during summer months and the herb festival each June.

Enjoying both planted and natural landscaping is possible at Dorflinger-Suydam Wildflower Sanctuary in White Mills. Summer outdoor concerts bring hundreds of listeners to enjoy live music. But I visited on a quiet day to hike the grounds explored by the sons of Christian Dorflinger when his family moved here to Wayne County from New York in 1862. Walking around Trout Lake and over meadows into a quiet woods, I found a spread of fringed polygala, a delicate fuchsia wildflower. Birdsong filled the spring-scented air.

This acreage was once the most important glass manufacturing company in the country. The former home of Christian Dorflinger is now a museum displaying the exquisite crystal that his factory made for presidents and kings until it closed in 1921. He brought artisans from England, France, Bohemia, and Sweden to cut, etch, and blow the famed Dorflinger glass. Of course, the museum's gift shop does not sell it, but the decorative glass offered is of fine quality.

A naturally scenic view of farmlands and mountains includes the French Azilum, a historic site along the Susquehanna River that was never fully occupied as intended. In 1793, French noblemen acquired 1,600 acres in Bradford County and mapped out a town grid. They then built more than 50 log houses for refugees who were fleeing the fury of the French Revolution. Not one structure of this wilderness asylum remains. On the site in Durell, a lively self-guiding tour with a video of a replica village retells this romantic rescue effort. From the Marie Antoinette Lookout along U.S. Route 6, a few miles west of the landmark Wyalusing Rocks, one can look down to the French Azilum 500 feet below.

The need for this safe haven fizzled when, at the end of the war in France, Napoleon Bonaparte grant-ed royalty the opportunity to return to their lands. A few did remain in Pennsylvania, and it is worthwhile to visit the LaPorte House, which was built in 1836 by a second generation Frenchman who was a surveyor.

Much farther north, two people put down roots and left a national legacy in their respective fields. In 1905, Zane Grey abandoned dentistry in New York and began writing top-selling westerns in his home in Pike County where the Lackawaxen and Delaware rivers meet. Visitors to the Zane Grey Home and Museum in Lackawaxen can learn about the varied adventures of this individualist and see the setting where he launched a career that earned him more than $37 million from 89 novels.

Also in Pike County, but in Milford, is the home of another national contributor with a commanding view–Grey Towers. In this country estate, young Gifford Pinchot developed a commitment to forestry, a field virtually unknown in America in the late 1800s. After adding a practical approach to years of European study, in 1905 Pinchot became the first chief of the new U.S. Forest Service. With support from President Teddy Roosevelt, he more than quadrupled the number of wooded acres set aside by the Forest Service. At Grey Towers, Pinchot formulated a natural resources commitment that made him "the father of American conservation." The mansion with careful restoration gives visitors a peek into how Gifford and his philanthropic liberal-thinking wife, Cornelia Bryce, entertained during his two terms as a Pennsylvania governor, which ended in 1935.

Long gone is time when residents joked that area attractions in the coal counties were limited to unsightly culm banks and barhopping. Many a visitor to Schuylkill County does stop at Yuengling's, America's oldest brewery, where a guide explains the process of brewing brought in 1829 by the German family that still runs this Pottsville operation.

Whether historical, industrial, or scenic, this region's attractions provide information and enjoyment in a wide variety of settings.

LEFT: *The JEM Classic Car Museum in Andreas (Schuylkill County) displays finely restored classic and antique automobiles, e.g., a 1931 Reo Royale Victoria (left) and 1929 Graham-Paige. John E. Morgan, owner of a knitting mill in Hometown, developed the collection.* **BELOW**: *At Quiet Valley Living Historical Farm near Stroudsburg, children grades three and up can enjoy lessons in a one-room school. Summer visits reveal many more 19th century farm experiences.* **BELOW LEFT**: *Greystone Towers (1886), the former country estate of Gifford Pinchot (1865-1946), consists of 41 rooms and 100 acres which include virgin white pine and hemlock forests in Milford, Pike County. Called the father of American conservation by late President John F. Kennedy, Pinchot served as chief of the United States Forest Service until 1910.* **BELOW FAR LEFT**: *Artist G.E. Mohler pens ink drawings for patrons at the Montage Mountain Art and Garden Festival.*

FAR LEFT: *The Northeastern Pennsylvania Philharmonic performs at the F.M. Kirby Center for the Performing Arts in Wilkes-Barre.* **LEFT:** *Lehighton's Pocono Museum Unlimited displays 16 moving 0-scale trains in a countryside with industries, highways with moving cars, and lighted communities with a lake and an amusement park.* **BELOW RIGHT:** *Among numerous antique dealers across the region, Carriage House Antiques near Clarks Summit shows several floors of restored antiques in two 19th century barns put together. (Lackawanna County)* **BELOW LEFT:** *Zane Grey Museum in Lackawaxen (Pike County) is the home where a New York dentist settled and became a successful novelist of Westerns. A tour inspires ponderings of American individualism.*

ABOVE: *Among the top names in entertainment, the Spice Girls perform at the Montage Performing Arts Center on Montage Mountain.* **LEFT:** *Handling concert audiences and sports fans up to 10,000, the First Union Arena at Casey Plaza is the home of the Wilkes-Barre/Scranton Penguins, the American Hockey League affiliate of the Pittsburgh Penguins.*

TOP RIGHT: *Each summer baseball fans go to the Lackawanna County Stadium to watch the Red Barons, the AAA team of the Philadelphia Phillies.* **BOTTOM RIGHT:** *Heading out with the day's catch completes a relaxing time fishing on the lake at Frances Slocum State Park in Luzerne County.* **BELOW:** *Tent camping is one of the recreational activities that attracts vacationers to the region's 18 state parks, here at World's End, a 780-acre state park with 70 campsites, Sullivan County.*

LEFT: *Bridal Veil Falls is one of seven breathtaking cascades that hikers enjoy on a 1.5 mile trail at privately-owned Bushkill Falls (Monroe County).* **BELOW AND BOTTOM**: *Since 1989, the Dorflinger Glass Museum has displayed some of the extraordinary crystal produced by the glass works of Christian Dorflinger and Sons at White Mills (Wayne County). Visitors can learn about the prolific output of cut and decorated glass by several hundred workers here at the turn of the 20th century and continuing to 1921.* **BELOW LEFT**: *Lake beach outings inflate the summer swimming crowd at Beltzville Lake in Beltzville State Park, a flood control project engineered in 1972 in Carbon County.*

TOP: *Located in Monroe County, the Pocono Indian Museum tells the story of the Lenapes.* **ABOVE LEFT:** *At the Old Mill Village Museum in New Milford, Susquehanna County, visitors relive the rich heritage of the Endless Mountains at the turn of the century.* **ABOVE RIGHT:** *The home of one of the earliest settlers in the Wyoming Valley, the Nathan Denison House was constructed in 1790 along Abrams Creek, Forty Fort, Luzerne County.* **RIGHT:** *Completed in 1807, Forty Fort Meeting House was used by many denominations.* **PAGES 138-139:** *Kazka, a Ukrainian dance ensemble, performs at Patch Town Days, an annual summer weekend at Eckley Miners' Village (Luzerne County).*

RIGHT: *A restored 19th century mill on Sawkill Creek offers educational, dining, and shopping experiences at the Jervis Gordon Grist Mill Historic District in Milford, Pike County.* FAR RIGHT: *Three of Pennsylvania's nine Heritage Regions, which promote tours of industrial sites and scenic byways, wind through the northeastern quadrant of the state. This marker and a taped guide direct visitors to historic canal and mining spots.* BELOW: *P.J.'s Farm Market Garden Center on U.S. Route 6 between Hawley and Lake Wallenpaupack exemplifies the productiveness of local farms and greenhouses.*

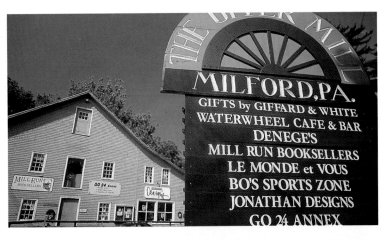

THE UPPER MILL
MILFORD, P.A.
GIFTS by GIFFARD & WHITE
WATERWHEEL CAFE & BAR
DENEGE'S
MILL RUN BOOKSELLERS
LE MONDE et VOUS
BO'S SPORTS ZONE
JONATHAN DESIGNS
GO 24 ANNEX

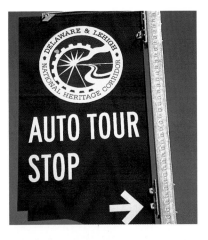

DELAWARE & LEHIGH
NATIONAL HERITAGE CORRIDOR

AUTO TOUR
STOP →

ABOVE: *A rail excursion between Steamtown National Historic Site in Scranton and Moscow is 26 miles round trip, following the former main line of the Delaware, Lackawanna and Western Railroad.* **LEFT**: *Since 1999 visitors to Steamtown can tour a restored railway post office (RPO), the Louisville and Nashville RPO No. 1100. Each RPO was a self-contained traveling post office staffed by postal clerks. The last RPO ran until 1977.*
FAR LEFT: *A cutaway exhibit in Steamtown's Technology Museum exposes the interior structure of a steam locomotive, the Spang-Chalfont & Co. #8 built by the Baldwin Locomotive Works in 1923.*

READING SOURCES

Anthracite Coal in Pennsylvania: An Industry and a Region. Mayfield: Lackawanna Heritage Valley Authority, 1997. A 100-page well-researched summary of the history of hard coal from its discovery to its decline as an economic force.

Bartoletti, Susan Campbell. **Growing Up in Coal Country.** Boston: Houghton Mifflin Co., 1996. A memoir that gives insight into the cultural milieu of Pennsylvania's northeast.

Clark, Kenneth R. and Janet Bregman-Taney. **The Insiders' Guide to the Pocono Mountains.** Stroudsburg: Pocono Record, 1997. A comprehensive manual to sites and services within Monroe, Carbon, Pike, and Wayne counties-apropos for residents and visitors.

Davies, Edward J., II **The Anthracite Aristocracy: Leadership and Social Change in the Hard Coal Regions of Northeastern Pennsylvania, 1800-1930.** An in-depth look at the economic fabric of hard coal, e.g., mine owners and investors in related industries.

Hiddlestone, Jack and Maryellen Calemmo. **Wish you were here...A Picture Postcard History of Lackawanna County, PA.** Scranton: Lackawanna Historical Society, 1997. An chronological overview of the county as conveyed by postcards.

Klopfer, Tom. **Toponyms and Trivia of Northeastern Pennsylvania.** Olyphant: Dunmore Publishing, 1998. Small delights and unusual characteristics of the boroughs and hamlets in seven counties.

Miller, Donald L. and Richard E. Sharpless. **The Kingdom of Coal: Work, Enterprise and Ethnic Communities in the Mine Fields.** Philadelphia: University of Pennsylvania Press, 1985. A comprehensive history of hard coal and the regional culture surrounding it, including its impact on other industries, labor relations, human lives, and the environment.

Oplinger, Carl S. and Robert Halma. **The Poconos: An Illustrated Natural History Guide.** New Brunswick: Rutgers University Press, 1988. An in-depth handling of the natural resources resulting from geological action eons ago.

Serrao, John. **Nature's Events: A Notebook of the Unfolding Seasons.** Mechanicsburg: Stackpole Books, 1992. Descriptions of 48 of nature's most spectacular and reliable annual happenings in America's northeast by an observant naturalist residing in the Poconos.

Shalaway, Scott and Linda. **Quiet Water Canoe Guide, Pennsylvania: Best Paddling Lakes and Ponds for All Ages.** Boston: Appalachian Mountain Club Books, 1994. The Northeast Region portion of this guide by seasoned outdoor folks is useful for exploring the area's many lakes.

Weidensaul, Scott. **Seasonal Guide to the Natural Year/Mid-Atlantic.** Colorado: Fulcrum Publishing, 1992. Special places to enjoy nature in Pennsylvania's northeast are included within this month-by-month guide.

Zbiek, Dr. Paul J. **Luzerne County: History of the People and Culture.** Wilkes-Barre: Wyoming Historical and Geological Society, 1994. An illustrated historical perspective of the tradition and heritage of communities in Luzerne County.

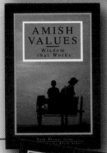

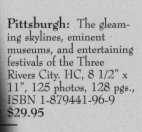